INTELLEGENDA

INTELLEGENDA

Comprehension Exercises in
Latin Prose and Verse

by

M.G. BALME
Assistant Master, Harrow School

OXFORD UNIVERSITY PRESS

1970

Oxford University Press, Ely House, London W. 1

GLASGOW NEW YORK TORONTO MELBOURNE WELLINGTON
CAPE TOWN SALISBURY IBABAN NAIROBI DAR ES SALAAM LUSAKA ADDIS ABABA
BOMBAY CALCUTTA MADRAS KARACHI LAHORE DACCA
KUALA LUMPUR SINGAPORE HONG KONG TOKYO

Printed in Great Britain by
Spottiswoode, Ballantyne and Co. Ltd.,
London and Colchester

CONTENTS

Introduction

It is generally agreed that the aim of a Latin course is to bring pupils as fast as possible to a stage where they can read Latin literature with some fluency and understanding. In such a course they will both learn about the ancient world through the words of the Romans themselves and experience something of one of the great literatures of the west. It must be admitted that the vast majority of pupils who abandon Latin at O level have failed to achieve these aims. This may be partly because O level syllabuses have concentrated too much on linguistic skills to the exclusion of intelligent understanding of what is read; in courses diluted by a shrinking allowance of time, linguistic skills have come to be regarded as an end in themselves. Great efforts are now being made to redress the balance and to make Latin once more an introduction to the humanities.

Amongst other experiments, the comprehension exercise, which has long been familiar in the teaching of English, is beginning to find a place and has already been introduced as a compulsory element in the O level examination of one board. It has the advantage of flexibility; attention can be directed towards sense, grammar, appreciation, background; it can make the pupil grapple with the meaning of passages as a whole, follow a line of argument and generally treat Latin with some critical intelligence.

This book contains about seventy short passages of prose and verse. These are grouped round twenty-one themes, most of which are concerned with perennial situations; some themes, such as slavery, are apparently alien to modern life but in these too there are aspects which are immediately familiar to us. The passages have been selected in the hope that they all fall within the actual or imaginative experience of a young reader today.

The book is meant to be used soon after real as opposed to made-up Latin is read, i.e. in or before the O level year. The principles of arrangement have made it hard to grade the passages in order of linguistic difficulty. The first three passages are heavily adapted. After this I have preferred to keep the original text with little alteration, making omissions to reduce the passages to manageable length. Generous help is given with vocabulary and linguistic difficulties on the page facing the text, but some rather hard passages occur early in the book, such as *Father and son* (from Horace, *Satire* vi), and teachers may wish to postpone or omit these.

Questions on the passages range from straightforward questions on narrative content to elementary critical questions, which are intended to provoke discussion. The questions on each passage generally start by following the narrative sentence by sentence and these can usually be answered precisely by reference to the text. The final questions are often wider and more open-ended; they may ask for a summary, or for a discussion of the writer's attitude to his subject, or for a comparison with contemporary situations. Even in the earliest exercises questions are asked which require a grasp of the passage as a whole and some evaluation of the characters concerned or the author's intention.

There is no hard and fast line between comprehension and critical questions. I have tried to avoid critical terminology and do not often ask about the writer's technique, but questions about the feeling and intention of a passage are basic. A passage is scarcely comprehended if the author's intention is mistaken, if, for instance, it is taken as serious when it is intended to be humorous. Although such questions may appear imprecise, some degree of precision can be achieved if answers are tied closely to the text; an answer which does not refer to or quote evidence from the Latin in support of a judgement is unsatisfactory.

Many of the exercises have been set for written answers and they work fairly well for this purpose, but they are intended primarily for oral use. The passages should not be translated before the questions are tackled. Understanding and translating a foreign language are different skills. It is possible to understand without translating. This is evident in the case of modern languages and is no less true of Latin, although the truth has been obscured by traditional methods of teaching. Translating without understanding is common not only in the early stages; even at a comparatively advanced stage a grammatically correct translation may betray a failure to understand what the writer means. Translation must always play an important part in any Latin course as the quickest way of checking rudimentary comprehension, as an exercise in transferring concepts from one language into another, and as a test of literary sensibility. But the habit of translating every word we read is I believe damaging. It impedes fluency, and by continually transferring Latin into inadequate English equivalents we fail to appreciate the nuances and sound and rhythm of the original.

Moreover, in English we read different books in different ways. We may skim a work of history for selected information or we may ponder a short poem for hours. It seems reasonable to apply similar techniques to reading Latin, sometimes reading fast with certain definite questions in mind, at other times reading slowly and squeezing the last drop of meaning from the text. This is not an open invitation to imprecision but an appeal to vary the reading lesson from an early stage.

Accurate understanding of the language is a prime objective but a flexible approach may bring pupils closer to intelligent understanding without loss of accuracy. If it served no other purpose, the comprehension exercise would be a useful variant on the routine reading lesson. The exercises in this book differ much in difficulty and could be taken at different speeds.

In tackling the exercises orally I should like to suggest the following as one possible procedure. The passage is first read aloud by the teacher, who will try to help the pupils understand the meaning by emphasis, tone of voice and pauses. At the first reading pupils will only take in part of the meaning and they should be encouraged to let their minds pass over what they fail to understand and concentrate on grasping as much of the story as they can; when the context is firmly established, gaps in understanding will more easily be filled. They may then be allowed to look at the help given on the page facing the text. Next, either the teacher or a pupil will read the passage aloud again. A simple prose passage should then be largely understood and, after the pupils have been allowed a few minutes to look it through on their own, the questions may be attempted. It is important not to start by treating the passage sentence by sentence; the passage as a whole should be grasped before any questions are attempted. The questions are not sacrosanct; teachers will wish to omit, add to or improve the questions given. A similar procedure may be followed with verse passages but, owing to the difficulties of vocabulary and word-order, comprehension is usually slower and it may be necessary to paraphrase a line in simpler Latin or ask for the translation of a few phrases.

To some passages I have appended a few questions on simple linguistic points. It could be fairly argued that if the passage has been well enough understood to answer the comprehension questions, grammatical questions of this kind are unnecessary. They may be omitted, but their purpose is to sharpen grammatical perception and to correct any tendency to treat a passage imprecisely when a translation is not demanded. To understand a language and to discuss its grammar are different operations and for this reason I have usually grouped the grammatical questions separately from the others. If pupils are not required to write Latin, knowledge of grammar means the ability to recognise quickly and accurately basic grammatical forms and syntactical structures in a Latin context. There are various ways of attaining this ability, including the structural approach, in which the language is learnt primarily by acquiring a grasp of Latin sentence patterns; but the complexity of Latin grammar and the multiplicity of ambiguous forms make analysis an essential tool, available when the flow of sense is blocked, and such analysis demands explicit discussion of grammatical forms and clausal structure. It is very properly unfashionable to teach grammatical labels to describe case usages etc. and I have tried to phrase the questions so that such labels are unnecessary; thus, in 2,i: 'Show the differences between the following usages of the ablative: *Roma, hoc tempore, infirma valetudine*', a good answer would be 'When you are away *from Rome*', '*At this time of year*', 'Since he was a man *of poor health*'. Similarly in 7,i: 'translate *Totum enim pollicerer, nisi timerem*; explain the use of the subjunctive': 'I would promise the whole sum, if I were not afraid ...'; the subjunctive is used because Pliny does not in fact promise the whole sum.'

In selecting passages on well-worn themes I have inevitably used many which have appeared in previous anthologies. I apologise to teachers who find them too familiar and hope they will be fresh to pupils. I have made considerable use of inscriptions which are strangely neglected in elementary Latin courses; I have referred to these by the numbers in Barrow, *Latin Inscriptions*, if they occur in that book. The comparison of Catullus 70 to the extract from Walter Scott *The Betrothed* is borrowed from Kennedy and Davis, *Two Centuries of Latin Poetry*.

Finally I should like to thank the pupils who have submitted to these exercises at the experimental stage and whose answers have enabled me to improve some of the questions, and friends who have read and criticised the manuscript, especially my colleague, J. H. W. Morwood.

1. A heroine and two heroes from early Roman history

i. Veturia

Coriolanus, a Roman, had gone over to the enemies of Rome and was about to lead them on an attack on the city when the following incident forced him to change his mind.

Veturia mater et Volumnia uxor duos parvos filios secum ferens in castra hostium procedebant et, quod armis viri urbem defendere non poterant, mulieres precibus et lacrimis defendebant. Ubi ad castra venerunt et nuntiatum est Coriolano ingens mulierum agmen adesse, 5
primum cognoscere noluit quae vellent. Deinde amicorum quidam, 'Nisi me fallunt oculi,' inquit, 'mater tua et coniunx et liberi adsunt.' Cum igitur Coriolanus ut matrem salutaret cucurrisset, mulier in iram ex precibus versa, 'Dic mihi,' inquit, 'utrum ad hostem an 10
ad filium venerim.'

LIVY ii, 40

1. Who were Veturia and Volumnia?
2. What were they doing?
3. Why were they doing this?
4. With which Latin words are *armis* and *viri* (l. 3) contrasted?
5. What was the first report Coriolanus heard about the action taken by Veturia and Volumnia?
6. What was his first reaction?
7. Who gave him further information? What was it?
8. What did Coriolanus do next? Why?
9. How did his mother react to this? What did she say?
10. What does the passage show about her character?

(i) In what case is each of the following words: *ferens* (l. 2); *armis* (l. 3); *Coriolano* (l. 5); *ingens* (l. 5)?

(ii) What part of what verb is each of the following forms and why is this part used: *adesse* (l. 5); *vellent* (l. 6); *dic* (l. 10)?

ii. Mucius Scaevola

Rome is being besieged by King Porsinna's army

'Transire Tiberim,' inquit, 'Patres, et intrare castra
hostium volo, non praedae causa neque ultionis. Maius
in animo est facinus.' Adprobant patres: abdito intra
vestem ferro proficiscitur. Ubi eo venit, in turba prope
5 regium tribunal constitit. Ibi cum stipendium militibus
forte daretur et scriba cum rege sedens simili veste multa
ageret, timens rogare uter Porsinna esset, ne se ipse
aperiret quis esset, scribam pro rege occidit. Vadentem
inde qua per trepidam turbam cruento mucrone sibi ipse
10 fecerat viam, comprehenderunt regii comites et retraxe-
runt. Tum quoque metuendus magis quam metuens,
'Romanus sum civis' inquit. 'C. Mucium me vocant.
Hostis hostem occidere volui, nec ad mortem minus
animi est quam fuit ad caedem; et facere et pati fortia
15 Romanum est.'

LIVY ii, 12

l. 2 *ultio, ultionis:* 'vengeance'.
l. 3 *abdere:* 'to hide'.
l. 5 *regium tribunal:* 'the royal platform' *stipendium:* 'pay'.
l. 6 *scriba:* 'secretary'.
l. 9 *mucro, mucronis:* 'sword point'.
ll. 13–14 *nec minus animi est:* 'and I have no less courage'.

1. Who is speaking the opening lines, and to whom?
2. What is the *maius facinus* (ll. 2–3)?
3. What was happening when he arrived in the enemy camp?
4. Why was he unable to distinguish the king from the secretary? Why did he not ask?
5. What was the result of his ignorance?
6. Describe the events immediately following the murder.
7. *metuendus magis quam metuens* (l. 11): explain these words and give a neat translation of them.
8. Explain the meaning of the last words of Mucius' speech. (*et facere et pati Romanum est* (ll. 14–15).) With which words in lines 13–14 do *facere* and *pati* respectively link up?
9. Which of the following best characterizes this speech: rash, nervous, desperate, defiant, silly?
10. What impression of Mucius does the author wish to give?

(i) Distinguish: *eo* (l. 4), *ibi* (l. 5), *inde* (l. 9).
(ii) Write out in Latin the sentence *Ibi cum ... occidit.* Bracket off the subordinate clauses, underline the main clause. How is the sentence constructed so as to make the most important fact prominent?

3

iii. Regulus

Carthaginienses Regulum ducem Romanum, quem
ceperant, petierunt ut Romam proficisceretur et pacem
a Romanis obtineret ac permutationem captivorum
faceret. Ille Romam cum venisset, inductus in senatum
5 nihil quasi Romanus egit, dixitque se ex illa die qua in
potestatem Afrorum venisset, Romanum esse desiisse.
Itaque et uxorem a complexu removit et Romanis suasit
ne pax cum Poenis fieret: illos enim fractos tot casibus
spem nullam habere; se tanti non esse ut tot milia
10 captivorum propter unum se et senem et paucos, qui ex
Romanis capti erant, redderentur. Itaque obtinuit; nam
Afros pacem petentes nullus admisit; ipse Carthaginem
rediit, offerentibusque Romanis ut eum Romae tenerent,
negavit se in ea urbe mansurum esse, in qua, postquam
15 Afris servierat, dignitatem honesti civis habere non
posset. Regressus igitur ad Africam omnibus suppliciis
exstinctus est.

Eutropius ii, 23

l. 3   *permutatio:* 'an exchange'.
l. 5   *quasi:* 'like'.
l. 6   *desinere, desii:* 'to cease'.
l. 7   *complexus -us:* 'embrace'.
l. 9   *tanti sum:* 'I am worth so much'.
l. 12   *admittere:* 'to let in'.
l. 15   *servire:* 'to be a slave to'.
l. 16   *supplicium:* 'torture'.

1. What did the Carthaginians ask Regulus to do (three things)?
2. When he came before the senate, how did he behave? Why did he act like this?
3. To whom do *Afrorum* (l. 6) and *Poenis* (l. 8) refer?
4. How did he treat his wife?
5. Give a translation of Regulus' speech *illos . . . redderentur* (ll. 8–11) in his actual words.
6. How was his advice received?
7. What did the Romans offer to do for him?
8. Why did he refuse this offer?
9. What happened to him on his return?
10. What had been Regulus' position in Africa before he was captured? How old was he? What qualities of his character does the passage show? Do you admire his behaviour?

(i) In what case is each of the following words: *qua* (l. 5); *tanti* (l. 9); *petentes* (l. 12); *Romae* (l. 13)?

(ii) From what Latin verb is each of the following nouns formed: *permutatio, potestas, casus?*

2. Home

i. Arpinum

Cicero has brought his friend Atticus to visit his birth-place, Arpinum, a small hill town about sixty miles south east of Rome.

ATTICUS: Antea mirabar te tam valde hoc loco delectari: nunc contra miror te, cum Roma absis, usquam potius esse.

CICERO: Ego vero, cum licet plures dies abesse, prae-
5   sertim hoc tempore anni, et amoenitatem hanc et salubritatem sequor: raro autem licet. Sed me alia quoque causa delectat, quae te non attingit ita.

ATTICUS: Quae tandem ista est?

CICERO: Quia, si verum dicimus, haec est mea et fratris
10   mei germana patria: hinc orti stirpe antiquissima sumus: hic sacra, hic genus, hic maiorum multa vestigia. Hanc vides villam, ut nunc quidem est, latius aedificatam patris nostri studio; qui, cum esset infirma valetudine, hic fere aetatem egit in litteris. Sed hoc
15   ipso in loco, cum avus viveret et antiquo more parva esset villa, me scito esse natum. Quare inest nescioquid et latet in animo et sensu meo, quo plus hic locus fortasse delectet, siquidem etiam ille sapientissimus vir, Ithacam ut videret, immortalitatem scribitur
20   repudiasse.

CICERO, *de Legibus* II, 2–3

6

l. 1   *tam valde:* 'so much'   *delectare:* 'to please, delight'.

l. 5   *amoenitas:* 'natural beauty'   *salubritas:* 'healthiness' (hilly country was healthy, low-lying country unhealthy, especially in late summer when fever was common).

l. 7   *attingere:* 'to touch, concern'.

l. 10   *germanus:* 'true, real'   *stirps, stirpis* f.: 'stock, origin'.

l. 11   *sacra,* n. pl.: literally 'sacred things'; Cicero means family shrines etc.

l. 14   *valetudo, valetudinis* (f.): 'health'.

l. 14   *litterae:* 'literature'.

l. 16   *scito:* imperative of *scio.*

ll. 16–17   *Quare inest . . . sensu meo:* 'And so there is something deep down in my mind and feelings . . .'

l. 18   *siquidem:* 'since, seeing that'.

l. 18   *ille sapientissimus vir:* Odysseus is referred to.

1. What used to surprise Atticus? What surprises him now?
2. In Cicero's first speech, what reasons does he give for liking to come to Arpinum?
3. *hoc tempore anni* (l. 5): what time of year do you suppose he means?
4. Translate appropriately *raro autem licet* (l. 6). Why should this be so?
5. Explain what Cicero means by *germana patria* (l. 10).
6. What was the house like in the time of Cicero's grandfather? What did his father do to it?
7. Why did his father spend his life there, and how did he spend it?
8. What is Odysseus said to have done? Why does Cicero refer to this story?
9. Summarize Cicero's personal reasons for coming to Arpinum whenever he could.

(i) *alia causa* (ll. 6–7): what case do you suppose these words are in? How would ambiguity be avoided in speaking the words aloud?

(ii) Show the difference between the following uses of the ablative: *Roma* (l. 2); *hoc tempore* (l. 5); *stirpe antiquissima* (l. 10); *infirma valetudine* (ll. 13–14).

(iii) *ut nunc est* (l. 12), *ut videret* (l. 19): distinguish these uses of *ut.*

ii. Sirmio

Catullus' home was at Sirmio, a long, thin peninsular on lake Garda in the north of Italy. He has just returned from a year's service abroad, on the staff of the governor of Bithynia (northern Turkey).

Paene insularum, Sirmio, insularumque
ocelle, quascumque in liquentibus stagnis
marique vasto fert uterque Neptunus,
quam te libenter quamque laetus inviso,
5   vix mi ipse credens Thuniam atque Bithunos
liquisse campos et videre te in tuto.
o quid solutis est beatius curis,
cum mens onus reponit, ac peregrino
labore fessi venimus larem ad nostrum,
10   desideratoque acquiescimus lecto?
hoc est quod unum est pro laboribus tantis.
salve, o venusta Sirmio, atque ero gaude
gaudente, vosque, o Lydiae lacus undae,
ridete quidquid est domi cachinnorum.

CATULLUS 31

l. 1   *Paene insularum:* compare English 'peninsular'.

l. 2   *ocelle:* Catullus addresse Sirmio as *ocellus*, literally 'little eye', a term of affection, e.g. 'gem of all *paene insularum . . .*'

l. 2   *stagnum:* 'a pond'.

l. 4   *quam . . . libenter:* 'how gladly'.

l. 5   *mi = mihi   Thuniam:* the Thuni and the Bithuni were the two tribes which made up the people of Bithynia.

l. 7   *solutis curis:* literally 'than cares loosed' i.e. 'than laying down ones cares'.

l. 8   *peregrinus -a -um:* 'foreign'.

l. 10   *lectus:* 'bed'.

l. 11   *hoc est quod unum est pro . . . :* 'this is the one thing which makes up for . . .'

l. 12   *venustus -a -um:* 'lovely'   *erus:* 'master'.

l. 13   *Lydiae:* 'Etruscan'; the Etruscans, who had settled round lake Garda, were thought to have come originally from Lydia (Turkey).

l. 14   *ridete . . . cachinnorum:* 'laugh with all the laughter you have at your command'.

1. What is the contrast between *stagnis* and *mari* (ll. 2–3)? What is meant by *uterque Neptunus* (l. 3)?
2. Explain the meaning of the first three lines in simple terms.
3. Translate lines 5 and 6. Suggest why Catullus should say this.
4. Summarize the meaning of lines 7 to 10.
5. What metaphor is suggested by *solutis* (l. 7) and *onus* (l. 8)?
6. Explain what is meant by *larem nostrum* (l. 9). With which phrase are these words contrasted?
7. What does Catullus tell Sirmio to do and what does he mean by telling the waves to laugh?
8. In this poem how does Catullus appear to feel about his year's service in Bithynia? Describe the feelings he has on his return home, quoting the Latin words and phrases which support your answer.
8. How far does the poem seem to you the natural expression of natural feelings? At what points, if any, does it seem to you artificial?
9. Read the poem aloud again. Verse composed in the metrical units $\cup - \cup -$ is called iambic. Scan lines 3, 4 and 7. Why should the verse in which this poem is composed be called 'limping iambics'?

iii. Rome

After the destruction of Rome by the Gauls (390 B.C.), there
was a proposal to move the site of the city. Camillus resisted
this proposal in a speech from which the following passage is
taken.

Nihilne nos tenet solum patriae nec haec terra quam
matrem appellamus, sed in superficie tignisque caritas
nobis patriae pendet? Equidem cum abessem, quotiens-
cumque patria in mentem veniret, haec omnia occur-
5 rebant, colles campique et Tiberis et adsueta oculis regio
et hoc caelum sub quo natus educatusque essem; quae
vos, Quirites, nunc moveant potius caritate sua ut
maneatis in sede vestra quam postea, cum reliqueritis
eam, macerent desiderio. Non sine causa di hominesque
10 hunc urbi condendae locum elegerunt, saluberrimos
colles, flumen opportunum, quo ex mediterraneis locis
fruges devehantur, quo maritimi commeatus accipi-
antur, mari vicinum ad commoditates nec expositum
nimia propinquitate ad pericula classium externarum,
15 regionum Italiae medium, ad incrementum urbis natum
unice locum.

LIVY v, 54

l. 1   *solum patriae:* 'our country's soil'.

ll. 2–3   *in superficie tignisque . . . pendet:* 'depends upon buildings and materials'   *caritas:* 'dearness, affection'.

l. 3   *equidem:* 'I for my part'.

l. 3   *abessem:* Camillus had been in exile at the time of the Gallic invasion but had been recalled, had been elected dictator and had defeated the Gauls.

ll. 4–5   *occurrere:* 'to occur (to mind)'.

l. 5   *adsueta oculis regio:* literally 'the district accustomed to my eyes' i.e. 'the country my eyes were used to'.

l. 9   *macerent desiderio:* 'torment you with longing'.

l. 10   *saluber:* 'healthy'.

l. 11   *mediterraneis:* 'inland'.

l. 12   *commeatus -us:* 'supplies, goods'.

l. 13   *commoditas:* 'advantage, convenience'.

l. 14   *externus -a-um:* 'foreign'.

l. 15   *ad incrementum . . . locum:* 'a place uniquely formed for a city's growth'.

1. Translate into idiomatic English *in superficie . . . pendet* (ll. 2–3). Explain the point of the opening sentence.
2. When Camillus thought about his country in exile, what used he remember?
3. Who are the *Quirites* (l. 7)? What does Camillus hope for them?
4. With which Latin words are *moveant caritate* (l. 7) contrasted?
5. Explain the meaning of *nec expositum . . . externarum* (ll. 13–14).
6. Summarize the advantages which Camillus claims for the site of Rome.
7. Camillus' appeal is addressed partly to sentiment, partly to reason. Explain the distinction and list the phrases which are intended mainly to rouse the feelings of the audience.
8. 'Rhetoric' may be defined as the art of persuasion. How does the last sentence of the passage exemplify this art (consider both the content and the arrangement of the content)?
9. Which of the advantages claimed for the site of Rome could also be claimed for the site of London?

iv. Flight from home

The Greeks have taken Troy and the city is burning. Anchises, Aeneas' father, at first refused to leave, but, in the lines immediately preceding, he has at last consented to go.

Dixerat ille, et iam per moenia clarior ignis
auditur, propiusque aestus incendia volvunt.
'ergo age, care pater, cervici imponere nostrae;
ipse subibo umeris nec me labor iste gravabit;
5   quo res cumque cadent, unum et commune periclum,
una salus ambobus erit. mihi parvus Iulus
sit comes, et longe servet vestigia coniunx.
tu, genitor, cape sacra manu patriosque penates.'
   Haec fatus latos umeros subiectaque colla
10 veste super fulvique insternor pelle leonis,
succedoque oneri; dextrae se parvus Iulus
implicuit sequiturque patrem non passibus aequis;
pone subit coniunx. ferimur per opaca locorum,
et me, quem dudum non ulla iniecta movebant
15 tela neque adverso glomerati examine Grai,
nunc omnes terrent aurae, sonus excitat omnis
suspensum et pariter comitique onerique timentem.

               VIRGIL, *Aeneid* ii. 705–729 (with omissions)

l. 2   *aestus -us:* 'heat'.

l. 3   *ergo age:* 'come on, then'   *cervix, cervicis, f:* 'neck'
imponere: 'place yourself' (imperative).

l. 4   *umerus:* 'a shoulder'   *gravare:* 'to weigh down'.

l. 5   *quo . . . cumque:* 'however'   *communis -e:* 'common,
shared'.

l. 7   *longe servet vestigia:* 'follow my tracks at a distance'.

l. 8   *genitor:* 'father'   l. 9 *colla -orum:* 'neck'.

l. 10   *fulvus -a-um:* 'yellow, tawny'   *pellis:* 'skin'   *insternor:* 'I
cover'.

l. 11   *succedo:* 'I bend to'   *se implicare:* 'to attach himself, catch
hold of'.

l. 13   *pone:* 'behind'   *feror:* 'I am carried, I rush'   *opaca
locorum:* 'dark places'.

l. 14   *dudum:* 'just now'.

l. 15   *glomerati:* 'close packed'   *examen -inis:* a 'swarm'.

l. 16   *aura:* 'breeze'.

l. 17   *suspensus:* 'anxious, in suspense'.

1. In what ways is the danger from the fire stressed?
2. What does Aeneas tell his father to do? Which phrases later in the passage show us that these instructions are being carried out?
3. *nec me labor iste gravabit* (l. 4): why does Aeneas say this?
4. What does he tell Iulus and his wife to do?
5. What do you understand by *sacra patriosque penates* (l. 8)? Why do you suppose they were so important?
6. Describe what Aeneas does in lines 9 and 10.
7. What is the picture given by *dextrae se . . . passibus aequis* (ll. 11–12)?
8. How had Aeneas felt in battle and how does he feel now? What has caused this change of spirit?
9. Collect all the phrases in the passage which express the love and concern of Aeneas for his father.
10. Read the passage in Latin again; then, without looking at the text, describe in your own words how Aeneas and his family left their home.

3. Husbands and wives

i. Pliny and Calpurnia

C. Plinius Calpurniae suae S.

Incredibile est quanto desiderio tui tenear. In causa amor primum, deinde quod non consuevimus abesse. Inde est quod magnam noctium partem in imagine tua
5 vigil exigo; inde quod interdiu, quibus horis te visere solebam, ad diaetam tuam ipsi me pedes ducunt; quod denique aeger et maestus ac similis excluso a vacuo limine recedo. Unum tempus his tormentis caret, quo in foro et amicorum litibus conteror. Aestima tu, quae vita
10 mea sit, cui requies in labore, in miseria curisque solacium. Vale.

PLINY, *Ep*. VII, 5

l. 1 *S.:* an abbreviation for *salutem dat:* 'sends greetings' (compare *S.D.* in the next letter).

l. 2 *incredibilis -e:* 'incredible' *desiderium:* 'longing' (for what is absent) *In causa amor primum:* 'the reason is first, love . . .'

l. 3 *consuevimus:* from *consuesco:* 'I am used to' *inde est quod:* literally, 'from this is the fact that . . .' i.e. 'this is why'.

l. 4 *in imagine tua:* 'in thinking of you' (*imago = likeness*, picture, thought) *vigil:* 'awake' *exigo:* 'I spend'.

l. 5 *interdiu:* 'in the day time'.

l. 6 *diaeta:* 'a room' *denique:* 'finally'.

l. 7 *maestus:* 'sad' *similis excluso:* 'like (a lover) shut out' (*excludo*) *limen, liminis:* 'door, room' *recedo:* 'I go back, withdraw'.

l. 8 *tormentum:* 'torture, misery' *careo:* 'I lack, am free from' (with ablative) *in foro:* the *forum* was the centre of public life and the law courts *lites:* 'law suits'.

l. 9 *contero:* 'I wear out' *aestimare:* 'to judge'.

l. 10 *solacium:* 'comfort, relief'.

1. Translate the first sentence into natural English.
2. What reasons does Pliny give for missing Calpurnia?
3. What three symptoms of his state of mind does he describe?
4. What was Pliny's business or profession? Where was he living when he wrote this letter? Which words show you?
5. Explain the point of the last sentence, especially *cui requies . . . solacium*; what would be meant by calling this clause a paradox?
6. Give a short commentary on this letter, reconstructing the circumstances as far as you can and summarizing Pliny's feelings.

ii. Cicero and Terentia

Tullius S.D. Terentiae suae

In Tusculanum nos venturos putamus aut Nonis aut postridie: ibi ut sint omnia parata—plures enim fortasse nobiscum erunt et, ut arbitror, diutius ibi commorabi-
5 mur: labrum si in balineo non est, ut sit: item cetera quae sunt ad victum et ad valetudinem necessaria. Vale.
Kal. Oct. de Venusino

CICERO, *ad Fam.* xiv, 20

iii. An epitaph

This epitaph from Rome is inscribed on a statue of a man and a woman; the woman stands holding the man's right hand with both her own.

Lucius Aurelius Lucii libertus Hermia lanius de colle Viminali.
> Haec quae me fato praecessit, corpore casto
> coniunx una, meo praedita amans animo,
> fido fida viro vixit studio parili, cum
5 > nulla in amaritie cessit ab officio.
> Aurelia Lucii liberta.

Dessau 7472 from Rome *c.* 80 B.C.

l. 2 *Tusculanum:* Cicero's house at Tusculum near Rome
Nonis: i.e. on 7th October.
l. 3 *ibi ut sint:* supply e.g. *fac,* 'see that . . .'
l. 5 *labrum:* 'a basin, tub'   *balineum:* 'the bath room'.
ll. 5–6 *item:* 'likewise, also'   *victus -us:* 'food, sustenance'.
l. 7 *Venusinum:* Cicero's house at Venusia in the south of Italy.

1. What information does Cicero give Terentia in the first
   sentence?
2. What preparations does he tell her to make, and why?
3. Account for the difference in grammatical mood of *ut sint*
   (l. 3) and *ut arbitror* (l. 4).
4. How do you think Terentia would have felt on receiving
   this letter? What features would have been especially
   aggravating?
5. Compare the tone of this letter with that of Pliny above.

l. 1 *Lucii libertus:* 'the freedman (i.e. freed slave) of Lucius'; so
in l. 7 *liberta*=freedwoman; on receiving their freedom slaves
usually took their master's names. *lanius:* 'a butcher'   *Viminalis:*
the Viminal was one of the seven hills of Rome.
l. 3 *castus:* 'chaste'.
l. 4 *meo praedita animo:* literally 'possessed of my heart' i.e.
'mistress of my heart'.
l. 5 *amarities*=*amaritia* 'in no time of bitterness'   *cedere ab;* 'to
yield from, leave, give up'.

1. What do you learn from this epitaph about Lucius
   Hermia?
2. What does *quae me fato praecessit* (l. 3) mean?
3. What qualities does he ascribe to his wife?
4. Where does he make plain his own feelings for her?
5. What is the effect of juxtaposing *fido fida* (l. 4)?

3

4. The family

i. Father and daughter

Cicero writes to Terentia about Tullia

Tullius Terentiae suae S.D.

In maximis meis doloribus excruciat me valetudo
Tulliae nostrae, de qua nihil est quod ad te plura
scribam; tibi enim aeque magnae curae esse certe scio.
5 Quod me propius vultis accedere, video ita esse facien-
dum; etiam ante fecissem, sed me multa impediverunt,
quae ne nunc quidem expedita sunt. Sed a Pomponio
exspecto litteras, quas ad me quam primum perferendas
cures velim. Da operam ut valeas.

CICERO, *ad Fam*. xiv, 19

ii. Mother and daughter

D(is) M(anibus) S(acrum). Calliste vixit annis XVI
me(n)s(ibus) III hor(is) VI et s(emisse); nuptura idibus
Oct(obribus), moritur(ante diem) IIII idus Octobres:
Panathenais mater pia car(ae) fil(iae) fecit.

Barrow 144

Inscription on a tombstone from the Roman town of Tipasa
in Mauretania (North Africa). Abbreviations are much used
in Roman inscriptions; the letters in brackets do not appear
in this inscription

1 What seems to you the most touching feature in this
  inscription?
2 Only two words explicitly express emotion Which are
  they, and how do they differ in meaning?
3 Does the inscription seem to you to say too little, or too
  much, for its purpose?

l. 2 *doloribus:* Cicero had just returned from Greece, where he had been with Pompey's army, defeated by Caesar at Pharsalus *excruciare:* 'to torment'.

l. 4 *tibi . . . curae esse:* 'that you are equally worried'.

l. 5 *propius:* Terentia was in Rome, Cicero at Brindisi, in the south of Italy.

l. 7 *expedire:* 'to set right, arrange'.

l. 7 *Pomponius:* Titus Pomponius Atticus was Cicero's closest friend.

ll. 8–9 *perferre:* 'to deliver' *da operam:* 'take care'.

1. What is tormenting Cicero?
2. Why does he say no more on this subject?
3. *Quod . . . accedere* (l. 5): who is the subject of *vultis*? What do they want? What is Cicero's reaction to their wish?
4. Explain *etiam ante fecissem* (l. 6).
5. What bearing do you suppose Pomponius' letter might have had on the situation?
6. What does the letter show about Cicero's feelings towards Terentia and Tullia?

l. 1 *D(is) M(anibus) S(acrum):* 'sacred to the spirit of the departed' *annis:* the ablative, instead of the accusative case, is often used in inscriptions to express time how long.

l. 2 *semisse:* 'a half'.

l. 3 *idibus Octobribus:* 15th October.

iii. Father and son

The father of the poet Horace had been a slave, who achieved his freedom and then became an auctioneer's agent (*coactor*) and a small farmer. Horace wrote the following lines about him when he was already winning fame as a poet. In the preceding lines, he has said: 'If my character has no bad faults, if no one can accuse me truly of greed and dirty living, if I am liked by me friends . . .'

causa fuit pater his, qui macro pauper agello
noluit in Flavi ludum me mittere, magni
quo pueri magnis e centurionibus orti,
laevo suspensi loculos tabulamque lacerto,
5 ibant octonos referentes Idibus aeris:
sed puerum est ausus Romam portare, docendum
artes quas doceat quivis eques atque senator
semet prognatos. vestem servosque sequentes
in magno ut populo si qui vidisset, avita
10 ex re praeberi sumptus mihi crederet illos.
ipse mihi custos incorruptissimus omnes
circum doctores aderat. quid multa? pudicum,
qui primus virtutis honos, servavit ab omni
non solum facto, verum opprobrio quoque turpi;
15 nec timuit sibi ne vitio quis verteret, olim
si praeco parvas aut, ut fuit ipse, coactor
mercedes sequerer; neque ego essem questus: at hoc
    nunc
laus illi debetur et a me gratia maior.
nil me paeniteat sanum patris huius.

HORACE, Satires I, vi, 71–89

l. 1   *macro pauper agello:* 'a poor man with a little farm'.

l. 3   *orti:* literally 'sprung from'; 'sons of'.

l. 4   'with their satchel and slate hanging on their left shoulder'.

l. 6   *puerum:* supply *me*   *docendum:* 'to be taught . . .'

l. 7   *quivis eques:* 'any knight'; the knights were the social class second to the senators.

l. 8   *semet prognatos:* literally 'those born from himself', i.e. 'his sons'.

l. 9   *in magno ut populo:* 'in the crowd'.

l. 10   *sumptus -us:* 'expense'.

ll. 9–10   *avita ex re:* 'from an ancestral estate'.

l. 12   *quid multa?* literally 'why (should I say) much?', i.e. 'in short'   *pudicus:* 'pure'.

l. 13   *qui primus virtutis honos:* 'which is the crown of virtue'.

l. 14   *opprobrium:* 'scandal'.

l. 15   *sibi ne vitio quis verteret:* 'that someone might hold it against him'   *olim/si:* 'if one day . . .'

l. 16   *praeco:* 'an auctioneer'.

l. 17   *mercedes:* 'salary'   *hoc* (ablative): 'because of this'.

l. 20   *nil me paeniteat:* 'I should never be dissatisfied'.

1. What did Horace's father refuse to do? What did he dare to do? What was daring about this?
2. What does *magnus* mean in lines 2 and 3? (It might mean two things at the same time.)
3. Explain why they each took eight bronze pieces on the Ides. Was this a lot for this purpose?
4. Contrast the school of Flavius with that to which Horace's father sent him.
5. *vestem* (l. 8): what is implied about Horace's clothes? Why should this have mattered to him?
6. *ipse . . . aderat* (ll. 11–12): what did Horace's father do? Why did he do it? Who normally did this job for a wealthy Roman schoolboy?
7. *olim si praeco . . . sequerer* (ll. 15–17): why should anyone have held this against Horace's father?
8. *at hoc . . . maior* (ll. 17–19); explain what Horace means.
9. What is meant by *sanum* and *huius* (l. 20)?
10. Summarize the picture which Horace gives of his father.

iv. Mother and son

Mos antea senatoribus Romae fuit, in curiam cum
filiis introire. Olim cum in senatu res maior quaedam
consultata esset eaque in diem posterum prolata est,
placuit ne quis eam rem enuntiaret, priusquam decreta
5 esset. Mater Papirii pueri, qui cum parente suo in curia
fuerat, percunctata est filium, quid in senatu patres
egissent. Puer repondit tacendum esse neque id dici licere.
Mulier fit audiendi cupidior; quaerit igitur violentius.
Tum puer, matre urgente, lepidi mendacii consilium
10 capit. Actum esse in senatu dixit, utrum utilius reipub-
licae videretur ut unus vir duas uxores haberet, an ut una
apud duos nupta esset. Hoc illa ubi audivit, animus
compavescit, domo trepidans egreditur, ad ceteras
matronas perfert. Venit ad senatum postridie matrum
15 caterva. Lacrimantes atque obsecrantes orant ut una
potius duobus nupta fieret quam uni duae. Senatores
ingredientes in curiam, quae illa mulierum intemperies
et quid postulatio istaec vellet, mirabantur. Puer in
medium curiae progressus, quid mater audire institisset,
20 quid ipse matri dixisset, rem, sicut fuerat, narrat.

AULUS GELLIUS, i, 23

l. 1   *curia:* 'the senate house'.
l. 3   *consultare:* 'to discuss'   *proferre:* 'to adjourn'.
l. 4   *placuit ne quis . . . :* 'it was decided that no one . . .'
l. 6   *percunctari:* 'to question, cross examine'.
l. 7   *agere:* 'to discuss'.
l. 9   *lepidus:* 'witty'.
l. 9   *mendacium:* 'lie'.
l. 13   *compavescere:* 'to panic'.
l. 15   *caterva:* 'crowd'   *obsecrare:* 'to beseech'.
l. 16   *potius . . . quam:* 'rather . . . than'.
l. 18   *intemperies:* 'lunatic behaviour'.
l. 19   *instare:* 'to insist'.

1. What was the custom referred to in line 1?
2. What did the senate decide, and why?
3. What did his mother ask Papirius?
4. What did he reply?
5. What effect did his reply have on his mother?
6. What was Papirius' *lepidum mendacium* (l. 9)?
7. When his mother heard it, how did she feel? What did she do?
8. What did the crowd of women beg from the senate?
9. How did Papirius end the senators' surprise?
10. What is the writer's attitude to (a) Papirius (b) his mother?

(i) In what case is each of the following words and why is this case used: *senatoribus* (l. 1); *Romae* (l. 1); *domo* (l. 13); *caterva* (l. 15); *uni* (l. 16)?

(ii) *Hoc illa ubi audivit* (l. 12): parse *hoc* and *illa* and say to what each refers.

(iii) Write out in Latin the sentence *Mater Papirii . . . egissent* (ll. 5–7); bracket off subordinate clauses and underline the main clause.

23

5. Masters and slaves

i. A loyal slave

Vitalis, C. Lavi Fausti ser(vus), idem f(ilius), verna
domo natus, hic situs est: annos vixit XVI: institor
tabernae Aprianae, a populo acceptus, idem a dibus
ereptus. Rogo vos, viatores, si quid minus dedi mensurae
5 ut patri meo adicere(m), ignoscatis. Rogo per superos et
inferos ut patrem et matre(m) commendatos (h)abeatis.
Et vale.

From near Philippi, Barrow 160

ii. On the death of Erotion, a slave girl

Hanc tibi, Fronto pater, genetrix Flacilla, puellam
    oscula commendo deliciasque meas,
parvola ne nigras horrescat Erotion umbras
    oraque Tartarei prodigiosa canis.
5 impletura fuit sextae modo frigora brumae,
    vixisset totidem ni minus illa dies.
inter tam veteres ludat lasciva patronos
    et nomen blaeso garriat ore meum.
mollia non rigidus caespes tegat ossa nec illi,
10   terra, gravis fueris: non fuit illa tibi.

MARTIAL, v, 34

1. What does Martial ask his parents to do?
2. What picture is suggested by lines 3–4?
3. How old was Erotion when she died?
4. What picture is suggested by lines 7–8? What is the point
   of line 8 (*nomen . . . meum*)?
5. Paraphrase the last two lines. Do they suggest a different
   attitude to death?
6. Do you find this poem touching or sentimental or both?

l. 1 *idem filius:* literally 'the same man the son', i.e. 'also the (adopted) son   (l. 1) *verna -ae,* m.: a slave born in his master's home.

ll. 2–3 *institor tabernae Aprianae:* 'keeper of the Aprian shop'; Aprium was perhaps the name of a village   *acceptus a:* literally 'received by' i.e. 'popular with'.

l. 4 *dibus = dis.*

l. 4 *minus mensurae:* literally 'too little measure', i.e. 'under weight'.

l. 6 *commendatos habeatis:* literally 'should have entrusted (to you)' i.e. 'should look after'.

1. What does *hic situs est* (l. 2) mean?
2. Why should he appeal to *viatores* (l. 4)? What does he ask them to do?
3. Who is referred to as *patri meo* (l. 5)?
4. Explain *per superos et inferos* (ll. 6–7).
5. Reconstruct Vitalis' life and character, as far as the inscription makes this possible.
6. What can you deduce from it about the relations of master and slave?

l. 1   Fronto and Flacilla, Martial's father and mother (*genetrix*), were already dead.

l. 2 *oscula deliciasque meas:* 'my sweetheart and my darling'.

l. 3 *parvolus -a -um:* 'poor little'.   *horrescere:* 'to tremble at'.

l. 4 *prodigiosus -a -um:* 'monstrous'.

l. 5 *implere:* 'to fulfil, complete'.   *bruma -ae:* 'winter'.

l. 6 'unless she had lived for as many (i.e. six) days less'.

l. 7 *lascivus -a -um:* 'playful'.   *patronos:* 'patrons, protectors', i.e. Fronto and Flacilla.

l. 8 *blaesus -a -um:* 'lisping'.   *garrire:* 'to stammer'.

l. 9 *caespes:* 'turf'.   *os, ossis, n.:* 'bone'.

iii. Slaves murder their master

Rem atrocem Larcius Macedo a servis suis passus est,
superbus alioqui dominus et saevus, et qui servisse
patrem suum parum, immo nimium, meminisset.
Lavabatur in villa Formiana. Repente eum servi circum-
5 sistunt. Alius fauces invadit, alius os verberat, alius pectus
et ventrem; et cum exanimem putarent, abiciunt in
fervens pavimentum, ut experirentur an viveret. Ille
sive quia non sentiebat, sive quia se non sentire simula-
bat, immobilis et extentus fidem peractae mortis
10 implevit. Tum demum quasi aestu solutus effertur;
excipiunt servi fideliores, concubinae cum ululatu et
clamore concurrunt. Ita et vocibus excitatus et recreatus
loci frigore, sublatis oculis agitatoque corpore, vivere se
(et iam tutum erat) confitetur. Diffugiunt servi; quorum
15 magna pars comprehensa est, ceteri requiruntur. Ipse
paucis diebus aegre focilatus, non sine ultionis solacio
decessit, ita vivus vindicatus ut occisi solent.

PLINY, *Ep.* III, xiv

l. 2 *alioqui:* 'in other respects, altogether'.

l. 2 *servire:* 'to be a slave'.

l. 3 *parum, immo nimium . . .:* 'too little, or rather too much . . .'

l. 4 *villa Formiana:* his house at Formiae, a sea-side resort on the bay of Naples.

l. 5 *fauces:* 'throat'.

l. 6 *venter:* 'stomach'.

l. 6 *exanimis:* 'lifeless'.

l. 7 *fervens:* 'burning hot'; the floor of the hot room of the baths would be heated.

l. 7 *an = num.*

ll. 9–10 *fidem peractae mortis implevit:* literally 'fulfilled belief in his death completed' i.e. 'made them believe that he was really dead'.

l. 10 *aestus -us:* 'heat'.

l. 11 *ululatus -us:* 'shrieks (of mourning)'.

l. 16 *aegre focilatus:* 'scarcely revived, just revived'.

l. 17 *vindicare:* to avenge.

1. What sort of master was Macedo?

2. What reason is suggested to account for his behaviour towards his slaves?

3. Describe the attack on Macedo. What feelings does Pliny's description evoke?

4. Why did the slaves think he was dead? What two reasons does Pliny suggest for his behaviour?

5. What made him come to? What evidence did he give of life?

6. What is the significance of *et iam tutum erat*?

7. What happened to him in the end?

8. What consolation did he have? Explain *ita vivus vindicatus ut occisi solent* (l. 18).

9. Where do you feel that Pliny's sympathies lie? (Your answer may not be simple; quote your evidence.)

(i) In the opening sentence the object comes before the subject. Suggest a reason for this word order.

(ii) In which sentences does the verb come before the subject? Suggest reasons for the order in each case.

(iii) *ut experirentur* (l. 7); *ut solent* (l. 17): distinguish these uses of *ut.*

27

iv. How to treat your slaves

Seneca writes to his friend, Lucilius

Libenter ex his qui a te veniunt cognovi familiariter
te cum servis tuis vivere. Hoc prudentiam tuam, hoc
eruditionem decet. 'Servi sunt.' Immo homines. 'Servi
sunt.' Immo contubernales. 'Servi sunt.' Immo humiles
5 amici. 'Servi sunt.' Immo conservi, si cogitaveris tantundem in utrosque licere fortunae ... Vis tu cogitare
istum quem servum vocas ex isdem seminibus ortum,
eodem frui caelo, aeque spirare, aeque vivere, aeque
mori? ... Haec tamen praecepti mei summa est: sic
10 cum inferiore vivas, quemadmodum tecum superiorem
velis vivere ... Vive cum servo clementer, comiter
quoque, et in sermonem illum admitte et in consilium et
in convictum ... Non est quod fastidiosi illi te deterreant
quominus servis tuis hilarem te praestes et non superbe
15 superiorem: colant potius te quam timeant ... Diutius
te morari nolo; non est enim tibi exhortatione opus.
Vale.

SENECA, *Ep.* 47 (abridged)

l. 1 *familiariter:* 'on friendly terms'.
l. 3 *eruditio:* 'learning, education'   *immo:* 'yes, but . . .'
l. 4 *contubernalis:* 'a comrade'.
l. 5 *conservus:* 'a fellow slave'.
l. 6 *tantundem in utrosque licere fortunae:* 'that fortune has the same power over both'   *vis tu?* literally 'are you willing to . . .?' i.e. 'please'.
l. 7 *semen, seminis:* 'seed'.
l. 8 *spirare:* 'to breathe'.
l. 9 *praeceptum:* 'advice, precept'   *summa, summae:* 'the sum'.
l. 11 *clemens:* 'gentle, kind'   *comis:* 'affable'.
l. 13 *convictus -us:* 'social life'   *fastidiosus:* 'proud, fastidious'.
l. 14 *hilaris:* 'cheerful'.
l. 15 *colere:* 'to respect'.

1 How does Lucilius treat his slaves?
2 What view does Seneca take of Lucilius' treatment of his slaves?
3 Why does *servi sunt* appear each time in inverted commas? What does Seneca mean by calling slaves *conservi* (l. 5)? Express in your own words Seneca's thought '*Servi sunt.*' *Immo homines . . . licere fortunae* (ll. 3–6).
4. What features common to slave and free does Seneca list in the sentence *Vis tu . . . mori* (ll. 6–9)? Sum the list up in one English phrase.
5. What is the summary of Seneca's advice? What English proverb does it recall?
6. What practical consequences follow from this precept, according to Seneca?
7. Which passage in the letter shows that such views would not have been universally acceptable?
8. To what situations in the contemporary world would the advice contained in this letter be applicable?

(i) To what does *hoc* (l. 2) refer?
(ii) In what cases are *fortunae* (l. 6) and *caelo* (l. 8), and why?
(iii) Distinguish the uses of the subjunctive *vivas* (l. 10) and *velis* (l. 11). Correct translation will show the distinction clearly.

6. Freedmen

i. How to get rich quick

The freedman Trimalchio tells his guests how he made his fortune.

Sed, ut coeperam dicere, ad hanc me fortunam frugalitas mea perduxit. Tam magnus ex Asia veni quam hic candelabrus est. Ad summam, cotidie me solebam ad illum metiri, et ut celerius rostrum barbatum haberem,
5 labra de lucerna ungebam. Ceterum, quemadmodum di volunt, dominus in domo factus sum. Quid multa? Coheredem me Caesari fecit, et accepi patrimonium laticlavium. Nemini tamen nihil satis est. Concupivi negotiari. Quinque naves aedificavi, oneravi vinum—et
10 tunc erat contra aurum—misi Romam. Omnes naves naufragarunt, factum non fabula. Uno die Neptunus trecenties sestertium devoravit. Putatis me defecisse? Alteras naves feci maiores et meliores et feliciores, ut nemo non me virum fortem diceret. Uno cursu centies
15 sestertium corrotundavi. Quidquid tangebam crescebat tamquam favus. Postquam coepi plus habere quam tota patria mea habet, manum de tabula: sustuli me de negotiatione et coepi per libertos faenerare.

PETRONIUS, *Satyricon* 75–6

(i) Distinguish the uses of ut: *ut coeperam dicere* (l. 1); *ut haberem* (l. 4); *ut nemo ... diceret* (ll. 13–14).

(ii) What is the difference between *alteras naves* (l. 13) and *alias naves*?

(iii) What is the force of the prefixes in the following words: *per-duxit* (l. 2); *con-cupivi* (l. 8); *de-voravit* (l. 12)?

l. 2   *frugalitas:* 'sterling qualities'.

l. 3   *candelabrus:* 'a lamp-stand; this might be a stand four or five feet high, supporting several oil lamps (*lucernae*).

l. 3   *ad summam:* 'in fact'.

l. 4   *metiri:* 'to measure'   *rostrum:* 'chin'   *barbatum:* 'bearded'.

l. 5   *labrum:* 'a lip'   *unguere:* 'to annoint'.

l. 6   *quid multa?* literally 'why much?' i.e. 'to cut a long story short'.

ll. 7–8   *Coheredem . . . laticlavium:* 'He (my master) made me co-heir with Caesar and I inherited a senator's fortune'; Trimalchio's master left half his fortune to the emperor and half to Trimalchio, which made him as rich as a senator.

l. 9   *negotiari:* 'to engage in business'.

l. 10   *contra aurum:* 'as precious as gold'.

l. 11   *naufragarunt:* 'were wrecked'.

l. 12   *trecenties sestertium:* 300,000 sesterces   *devorare:* 'to swallow up'   *deficere:* 'to give up'.

l. 15   *corrotundare:* 'to round off'.

l. 16   *tamquam favus:* 'like a honey comb'.

l. 17   *manum de tabula:* literally '(I took) my hand from the table' i.e. I downed tools, left off.

l. 18   *faenerare:* 'to lend money'.

1. What claim does Trimalchio make for himself in the first sentence? Does this characteristic emerge in his own account of what he did?

2. How big was he when he came from Asia?

3. What two uses did he make of the lamp-stand?

4. What did he decide to do when he inherited a fortune? What is meant by *nemini nihil satis est* (l. 8)?

5. What happened to his ships?

6. What did Neptune do? Translate appropriately *factum non fabula* (l. 11).

7. What quality did Trimalchio show at this point? How did this repay him?

8. At what stage did he retire from business?

9. How did he continue to make money?

10. Judging from this passage, what sort of a man was Trimalchio? Consider not only what he says but how he says it.

ii. A successful doctor

P. Decimus P. libertus Eros Merula, medicus clinicus,
chirugus, ocularius; VIvir. Hic pro libertate dedit HS $\overline{\text{L}}$.
Hic pro seviratu in rem publicam dedit HS $\overline{\text{II}}$. Hic in
statuas ponendas in aedem Herculis dedit HS $\overline{\text{XXX}}$.
5 Hic in vias sternendas in publicum dedit HS $\overline{\text{XXXVII}}$.
Hic pridie quam mortuus est reliquit patrimoni HS . . .

From Assisi, Barrow 147

iii. A surgeon's victim

D.M. Euhelpisti liberti: vixit annis XXVII mensibus
IIII dieb. XI:
florentes annos mors subita eripuit:
anima innocentissima, quem medici secarunt et occi-
5 derunt. P. Aelius Aug. lib. Pecularius alumno suo.

Barrow 149

32

l. 1 *Publii libertus:* 'the freedman of Publius'. His name was originally Eros; on being freed he took his master's name, P. Decimus Merula, in addition to his own. This was the usual practice. *clinicus:* 'physician'.

l. 2 *VIvir = sevir,* one of the six priests in charge of the local cult of the emperor. This was the highest honour a freedman could achieve.

l. 3 *HS $\overline{L}$:* 50,000 sesterces; *HS $\overline{II}$:* 2,000 sesterces

l. 4 *in aedem:* 'for the temple'.

l. 5 *sternendas: sternere* here means 'to lay (a road)', compare English 'street'.

l. 6 *patrimonii HS . . .:* 'an inheritance of . . . sesterces' (the figure is missing).

1. In what branches of medicine did Eros practise?
2. How did he achieve his liberty?
3. What public benefactions did he make?
4. His name, Eros, suggests a Greek extraction. How does the inscription show a slave of foreign origin becoming a useful, respected and patriotic Roman?
5. What does the inscription tell you of the means by which Roman towns were improved?

l. 1 *D.M. = dis manibus.*

l. 3 *anima:* 'soul, spirit'.

l. 5 *Aug. = Augustalis,* priest of Augustus, an alternative title for *sevir* (see above).

l. 5 *alumnus:* 'foster child'; a verb such as *fecit* must here be supplied—'he made this tomb for . . .'

1. Summarize the information given by this inscription.
2. Why is line 3 set out in this way? How does the language of this line differ from that of the rest of the inscription?
3. What features of the inscription particularly appeal to your sympathy?
4. What is unusual about the grammar of the following forms: *annis* (l. 1); *quem* (l. 4); *secarunt* (l. 4)?

4

iv. A nightmare doctor

Lotus nobiscum est, hilaris cenavit, et idem
　　inventus mane est mortuus Andragoras.
tam subitae mortis causam, Faustine, requiris?
　　in somnis medicum viderat Hermocratem.
MARTIAL vi, 53

v. A freedman from Parthia

　C. Iulius Mygdonius, genere Parthus, natus ingenuus,
captus pubis aetate, venumdatus in terram Romanam,
qui cum factus essem civis Romanus, iuvante fato,
collocavi arcam, dum essem annos L. Petii usque a
5　pubertate ad senectam meam pervenire; nunc recipe
me, saxe, libens; tecum cura solutus ero.
From RAVENNA, 1st century A.D.
Dessau 1980

1. How did Andragoras spend the evening before his death?
2. What caused his death?
3. What is the point of the epigram?

1. Summarize the information given about Mygdonius' life.
2. *nunc recipe me, saxe, libens:* explain what this means.
3. What is Mydonius' attitude to death? Why, despite his success, should he have felt like this?

7. Schools and schoolmasters

i. A noisy schoolmaster

Quid tibi nobiscum est, ludi scelerate magister,
    invisum pueris virginibusque caput?
nondum cristati rupere silentia galli:
    murmure iam saevo verberibusque tonas.
5 tam grave percussis incudibus aera resultant,
    causidicum medio cum faber aptat equo:
mitior in magno clamor furit amphitheatro,
    vincenti parmae cum sua turba favet.
vicini somnum non tota nocte rogamus:
10 nam vigilare leve est, pervigilare grave est.
discipulos dimitte tuos. vis, garrule, quantum
    accipis ut clames, accipere ut taceas?

MARTIAL ix, 68

ii. A class in action

Grais ingenium, Grais dedit ore rotundo
Musa loqui, praeter laudem nullius avaris.
Romani pueri longis rationibus assem
discunt in partes centum diducere. 'dicat
5 filius Albani: si de quincunce remota est
uncia, quid superat? poteras dixisse.' 'triens.' 'eu!
rem poteris servare tuam. redit uncia, quid fit?'
'semis.' an haec animos aerugo et cura peculi
cum semel imbuerit, speramus carmina fingi
10 posse linenda cedro et levi servanda cupresso?

HORACE, Ars Poetica 323–332

1. What claims does Horace make for the Greeks?
2. What do Roman boys learn at school?
3. What scene is painted in lines 4 to 8?
4. What is Horace's criticism of Roman education?

l. 2 *invisum . . . caput:* literally 'head hateful to' i.e. 'creature hated by'.

l. 3 *nondum:* 'not yet' *cristati . . . galli:* 'the crested cocks'.

l. 4 *verbera,* (n. pl.): 'blows' *tonare:* 'to thunder'.

l. 5 *grave:* adverb for *graviter* *incus, incudis:* 'an anvil' *aera* (n. pl.): 'bronze' *resultare:* 'to echo'.

l. 6 *causidicus:* 'a pleader, barrister' (*causam dicere*) *faber:* 'a smith'.

l. 7 *mitis:* 'soft, gentle'.	l. 10 *vigilare:* 'to lie awake'.
l. 8 *parma:* 'a shield'.	l. 11 *garrulus:* 'chatter-box'.

1. Summarize Martial's complaint.
2. What picture of the schoolmaster is built up in lines 1–4? Which Latin words particularly contribute to it?
3. The third couplet refers to a bronze-smith making an equestrian statue. How far has he got?
4. What is described in the fourth couplet?
5. From which words in line 4 do these comparisons develop, and what is their point?
6. How does the tone change in line 9? Scan the line. How does the rhythm help to express the change of tone?
7. What is the difference between *vigilare* and per-*vigilare* (l. 10)? How is this line given point?
8. How does the tone change again before the end of the poem? Which word clearly marks this change of tone?
9. Explain the meaning of the last sentence (*vis . . . taceas?*). On what note does the poem end?

l. 1 *Grai:* 'the Greeks'. *ore rotundo:* literally 'with rounded mouth', i.e. 'with polished style'.

l. 2 *nullius avaris:* 'greedy for nothing'.

l. 3 *as, assis:* a unit of weight and money divisible into twelve parts; *uncia* $=\frac{1}{12}$; *quincunx* $=\frac{5}{12}$ etc.

l. 6 *superare:* 'to be left'. *eu:* 'good!'

l. 7 *rem tuam:* 'your fortune'.

l. 8 *aerugo:* 'blight' *peculium:* 'cash'.

l. 9 *imbuere:* 'to stain, to taint'.

ll. 9–10 *carmina linenda . . . cupresso:* 'poems worth oiling with cedar oil and keeping in smooth cypress wood' (to preserve the books).

iii. The ideal schoolmaster

Sumat igitur ante omnia parentis erga discipulos animum, ac succedere se in eorum locum, a quibus sibi liberi tradantur, existimet. Ipse nec habeat vitia nec ferat. Non austeritas eius tristis, non dissoluta sit comitas,
5 ne inde odium hinc contemptus oriatur. Plurimus ei de honesto ac bono sermo sit; nam quo saepius monuerit, eo rarius castigabit. Minime iracundus, nec tamen eorum, quae emendanda erunt, dissimulator, simplex in docendo, patiens laboris, assiduus potius quam immo-
10 dicus. Interrogantibus libenter respondeat, non interrogantes percontetur ultro . . . Ipse aliquid, immo multa, cotidie dicat, quae secum auditores referant. Licet enim satis exemplorum ad imitandum ex lectione suppeditet, viva illa, ut dicitur, vox alit plenius praecipueque eius
15 praeceptoris, quem discipuli, si modo recte sunt instituti, et amant et verentur. Vix autem dici potest, quanto liberius imitemur eos, quibus favemus.

QUINTILIAN, *Institutio* II, ii, 5

l. 1   *erga:* 'towards'.

l. 4   *austeritas:* 'strictness'   *tristis:* 'joyless'   *dissolutus:* 'slack, lax'.

l. 4   *comitas, comitatis:* 'affability, friendliness'.

l. 6   *honestum:* 'what is honourable'   *quo . . . eo:* 'the more . . . the more . . .'

l. 8   *emendare:* 'to correct'   *dissimulator:* 'a concealer'.

l. 8   *simplex:* 'straightforward'   l. 9   *assiduus potius quam immodicus:* 'persistent rather than excessive' (in his demands for work).

l. 11   *percontari:* 'to question'   *ultro:* 'of his own accord'.

l. 11   *immo:* 'or rather'.

l. 12   *licet:* 'although'.

l. 13   *suppeditet:* 'are supplied'

l. 14   *alit plenius:* literally 'feeds more fully' i.e. 'supplies more satisfying food (for the mind)'.

l. 15   *praeceptor:* 'teacher'.

l. 15   *instituere:* 'to teach'.

1. According to Quintilian, what attitude should a school-master adopt towards his pupils?
2. Express *eorum a quibus tradantur* (ll. 2–3) by one Latin word.
3. Explain to what *inde* and *hinc* (l. 5) respectively refer.
4. Explain the meaning of *nec eorum . . . dissimulator* (l. 8).
5. Summarize the qualities recommended by Quintilian in the sentence *Minime iracundus . . . immodicus* (ll. 7–10).
6. What do you understand by *Ipse aliquid . . . referant* (ll. 11–12)?
7. What does *viva illa vox* mean, and with what is it contrasted?
8. In this passage, with what aspect of education is Quintilian mainly concerned? Support your answer by reference and quotation.
9. How far do you approve of this schoolmaster?

(i) To which word does *parentis* (l. 1) belong? Why is it in this position?

(ii) Why is *sumat* in the subjunctive? Where else in the passage is the subjunctive used with the same force?

(iii) From what verb is *dissimulator* (l. 8) formed? Find two other nouns in the passage formed in a similar way.

iv. Founding a school

C. Plinius Cornelio Tacito suo S.

Proxime cum in patria mea fui, venit ad me salutandum municipis mei filius praetextatus. Huic ego 'Studes?' inquam. Respondit: 'Etiam!' 'Ubi?' 'Medio-
5 lani.' 'Cur non hic?' Et pater eius (erat enim una atque etiam ipse adduxerat puerum): 'Quia nullos hic praeceptores habemus.' 'Quare nullos? Nam vehementer intererat vestra, qui patres estis' (et opportune complures patres audiebant) 'liberos vestros hic potissimum discere.
10 Ubi enim iucundius morarentur quam in patria aut pudicius continerentur quam sub oculis parentum aut minore sumptu quam domi? Quantulum est ergo collata pecunia conducere praeceptores, quodque nunc in habitationes atque in viatica impenditis, adicere mercedibus?
15 Atque ego, qui nondum liberos habeo, paratus sum pro re publica nostra, quasi pro filia vel parente, tertiam partem eius, quod conferre vobis placebit, dare. Totum etiam pollicerer, nisi timerem ne hoc munus meum quandoque ambitu corrumperetur, ut accidere multis in
20 locis video, in quibus praeceptores publice conducuntur . . . Atque utinam tam claros praeceptores inducatis, ut in finitimis oppidis studia hinc petantur, utque nunc liberi vestri aliena in loca ita mox alieni in hunc locum confluant!'

PLINY, *Ep.*, IV, xiii

l. 1　Pliny writes to Tacitus, the historian. *S. = salutem dat.*

l. 2　*proxime:* 'lately'　*patria mea:* i.e. his home town of Comum on lake Como, about twenty five miles north of Milan (*Mediolanum*). *ad me salutandum:* 'to pay his respects to me'; this refers to the early morning *salutatio*, at which distinguished Romans received visitors.

l. 4　*'studes?':* literally 'Are you studying?' i.e. 'Are you at school?' There would have been a primary school at Comum; the boy was of secondary school age (*praetextatus*).　*etiam:* 'yes'.

l. 5　*una* (adv.): 'with him'.

ll. 7–8　*vehementer intererat vestra:* 'it would be very much in your interest, it would be greatly to your advantage . . .'

l. 8　*opportune:* 'opportunely, luckily'.

l. 11　*continere:* 'to control'　*pudicus:* 'chaste, pure'.

l. 12　*quantulum:* 'how little'.

l. 13　*conducere:* 'to hire'.

l. 13　*habitationes:* 'lodgings' (for those boarding at school) *viatica*, n. pl.: 'journey money, fares'.

l. 14　*mercedes:* 'salary' (of the teachers).

l. 18　*polliceri:* 'to promise'　*quandoque:* 'at some time'.

l. 19　*ambitus -us:* 'bribery, graft'.

l. 20　*publice:* 'at public expense'.

ll. 22–3　*ut nunc . . . ita mox . . . :* 'as now . . . so soon . . .'

l. 24　*confluere:* 'to flock'.

1. Summarize the conversation between Pliny and his interlocutors in lines 3 to 7 (*huic ego . . . habemus*).
2. What three advantages does Pliny claim for having a school in his home town?
3. How does he suggest they should finance a school and make sure they get good teachers?
4. How much does he propose to contribute himself, and for what reasons?
5. Why does he not propose to contribute the whole cost?
6. What is Pliny's final wish for the proposed school?
7. What do you learn from this letter about the Roman system of education?
8. What do you learn about Pliny's character?

(i) Translate *Totum enim pollicerer, nisi timerem* (ll. 17–18): explain the use of the subjunctive.

(ii) Explain the use of the subjunctive *morarentur* (l. 10).

(iii) Distinguish the uses of *ut: ut . . . video* (ll. 19–20); *ut . . . petantur* (l. 22);

8. Three murders

i. A detective story

Hoc ipso fere tempore Strato ille medicus domi furtum fecit et caedem eius modi. Cum esset in aedibus armarium in quo sciret esse nummorum aliquantum et auri, noctu duos conservos dormientes occidit in piscinamque
5 deiecit; ipse armari fundum exsecuit et HS X et auri quinque pondo abstulit, uno ex servis puero non grandi conscio. Furto postridie cognito, omnis suspicio in eos servos qui non comparebant commovebatur. Cum exsectio illa fundi in armario animadverteretur, homines
10 quonam modo fieri potuisset requirebant. Quidam ex amicis Sassiae recordatus est se nuper in auctione quadam vidisse in rebus minutis tortuosam venire serrulam, qua illud potuisse ita circumsecari videretur. Ne multa, perquiritur a coactoribus, invenitur ea serrula
15 ad Stratonem pervenisse. Hoc initio suspicionis orto et aperte accusato Stratone, puer ille conscius pertimuit, rem omnem dominae indicavit; homines in piscina inventi sunt, Strato in vincula coniectus est, atque etiam in taberna eius nummi, nequaquam omnes, reperiuntur.

CICERO, *Pro Cluentio*, 179–80

l. 1 *ille:* Cicero has referred to Strato earlier in his speech.

l. 1 *furtum:* 'theft'.

l. 2 *armarium:* 'a chest, a safe'   *nummorum aliquantum:* 'a quantity of cash'.

l. 4 *piscina* 'a fish pond, cistern'   *fundus:* 'bottom'   *HS X:* 10,000 sesterces.

l. 6 *pondo* (indecl. noun): 'pounds'.

l. 7 *conscius:* 'in the know'.

l. 8 *comparere:* 'to appear, be evident'.

l. 11 Sassia was the mistress of the house.

l. 12 *res minutae:* 'trifling things, odds and ends'.

l. 12 *tortuosus:* 'twisted, curved'   *venire:* 'to be sold'   *serrula:* 'a little saw'.

l. 14 *ne multa:* supply *dicam;* literally 'not to say much' i.e. 'to cut a long story short'.

l. 14 *coactor:* 'an auctioneers's agent'.

l. 19 *taberna:* normally 'a shop'; here 'work-room, surgery' *nequaquam:* 'by no means'.

1. Who was Strato? What crimes did he commit?
2. Describe the successive steps by which he committed the crimes.
3. What accomplice did he have?
4. Who were suspected at first, and why?
5. What question puzzled the investigators?
6. What clue was given by a friend of Sassia?
7. How was this clue followed up?
8. What three things confirmed the case against Strato?
9. What mistakes would a cleverer criminal have avoided?

(i) Explain the function of the following pronouns: *ipso* (l. 1); *eius* (l. 2); *ipse* (l. 5); *ille* (l. 16).

(ii) Distinguish the following uses of the ablative: *hoc tempore* (l. 1); *uno . . . conscio* (ll. 6–7); *qua* (l. 13); *hoc initio* (l. 15).

(iii) *requirebant* (l. 10): which of the following translations is most appropriate: 'were asking', 'kept asking', 'began to ask'?

43

ii. Murder revealed by a dream

Cum duo quidam Arcades familiares iter una facerent et Megaram venissent, alter ad cauponem divertit, ad hospitem alter. Qui cum cenati quiescerent, visus est in somnis ei, qui erat in hospitio, ille alter orare, ut sub-
5 veniret, quod sibi a caupone interitus pararetur. Is primo perterritus somnio surrexit; dein cum se colle-gisset idque visum pro nihilo habendum esse duxisset, recubuit. Tum ei dormienti idem ille visus est rogare, ut, quoniam sibi vivo non subvenisset, mortem suam ne
10 inultam esse pateretur; se interfectum in plaustrum a caupone esse coniectum et supra stercus iniectum; petiit ut mane ad portam adesset, priusquam plaustrum ex oppido exiret. Hoc vero somnio commotus, mane bubulco ad portam obviam ivit, quaesiit ex eo quid esset
15 in plaustro; ille perterritus fugit, mortuus erutus est, caupo re patefacta poenas dedit.

CICERO, *de Divinatione* i, 56

l. 1 *Arcades:* 'Arcadians'; Arcadia is a district in Greece *familiaris:* 'a friend'.

l. 2 *Megaram:* a town *caupo, cauponis:* 'an innkeeper' *divertere:* 'to stay'.

l. 3 *hospes, hospitis:* literally 'a host' i.e. 'a friend'; compare *hospitium* (l. 4).

l. 5 *interitus:* 'death, murder'.

l. 6 *somnium:* 'a dream'.

l. 7 *pro nihilo habendum esse:* literally 'should be considered as nothing', i.e. 'was unimportant'.

l. 7 *ducere:* here means 'to think'.

l. 10 *inultus:* 'unavenged'.

l. 10 *plaustrum:* 'a cart'.

l. 11 *stercus, stercoris,* (n.): 'dung'   *mane:* 'in the morning'.

l. 14 *bubulcus:* 'a carter'   *obviam ire* + dative: 'to go to meet'.

l. 15 *eruere:* 'to dig up'.

1. What were the two friends doing? Where did each put up for the night?
2. Who appeared to whom in a dream?
3. What did the dream figure say?
4. How did the dreamer react at first?
5. What did he do next, and why?
6. Give the actual words of the dream figure in the second dream, translating into direct speech from *ut, quoniam* (l. 8) ... *iniectum* (l. 11).
7. How did the dreamer react to the second dream and what did he do?
8. What did the carter do?
9. What happened to the innkeeper?
10. Stories such as this are more likely to convince, if they give circumstantial detail. What detail of this kind does Cicero give? Does he give too much or too little for his purpose?

(i) In what case is each of the following words, and why: *Megaram* (l. 2); *qui* (l. 3); *sibi* (l. 5); *stercus* (l. 11); *patefacta* (l. 16)?

(ii) *mortem suam* (l. 9): what is unusual about the position of these words? Account for the word-order.

(iii) Write out in Latin *Qui cum* (l. 3) ... *pararetur* (l. 5); bracket off the subordinate clauses and underline the main clause.

iii. The murder of Sychaeus

Huic coniunx Sychaeus erat, ditissimus agri
Phoenicum, et magno miserae dilectus amore,
cui pater intactam dederat primisque iugarat
ominibus. sed regna Tyri germanus habebat
5 Pygmalion, scelere ante alios immanior omnes.
quos inter medius venit furor. ille Sychaeum
impius ante aras atque auri caecus amore
clam ferro incautum superat, securus amorum
germanae; factumque diu celavit et aegram
10 multa malus simulans vana spe lusit amantem.
ipsa sed in somnis inhumati venit imago
coniugis ora modis attollens pallida miris;
crudeles aras traiectaque pectora ferro
nudavit, caecumque domus scelus omne retexit.
15 tum celerare fugam patriaque excedere suadet
auxiliumque viae veteres tellure recludit
thesauros, ignotum argenti pondus et auri.
his commota fugam Dido sociosque parabat.

VIRGIL, *Aeneid* i, 343–360

46

l. 1 *huic:* refers to Dido. She was a princess of Tyre, a Phoenician city *ditissimus agri:* 'richest in land'.

l. 2 *magno . . . amore:* 'deeply loved by the unhappy (Dido)'.

l. 3 *intactam:* 'untouched', i.e. a virgin.

ll. 3–4 *primisque iugarat ominibus:* 'had united her with the first (marriage) omens' *germanus:* 'brother'.

l. 5 *immanis:* 'inhuman'.

ll. 8–9 *securus amorum germanae:* 'unconcerned about his sister's love'.

l. 10 *lusit:* 'deceived'.

l. 11 *inhumatus:* 'unburied' *imago:* 'ghost'.

l. 14 *nudare:* 'to lay bare' i.e. 'to reveal' *retegere:* 'to uncover'.

l. 16 *recludere:* 'to disclose'.

l. 17 *pondus, ponderis* (n.): 'weight'.

1. Who was Pygmalion? Express *scelere . . . omnes* (l. 5) in natural English.
2. To whom does *quos* (l. 6) refer? What do you understand by *furor*?
3. Describe the murder of Sychaeus. Why is *impius* (l. 7) especially appropriate, and how does Virgil give the word emphasis?
4. What was Pygmalion's motive?
5. How did he deceive Dido? Explain *vana spe* (l. 10)?
6. How did Dido find out the truth?
7. *ora . . . miris* (l. 12); what picture is given by this line?
8. *caecum scelus* (l. 14): what does *caecum* mean here? Where else in the passage do you find adjectives used in a poetic or unusual sense?
9. What did the ghost tell Dido to do, and what help did it give?
10. List all the words and phrases which describe the wickedness of Pygmalion and from this reconstruct his character.
11. What does this story have in common with the story in the preceding passage? Contrast the ways in which the stories are told, considering especially the details selected by each author.

9. Gladiators and gladiatorial shows

i. Seneca at a show

Casu in meridianum spectaculum incidi, lusus exspectans et sales et aliquid laxamenti quo hominum oculi ab humano cruore acquiescant. Contra est: quiquid ante pugnatum est, misericordia fuit; nunc
5 omissis nugis mera homicidia sunt. Nihil habent quo tegantur: ad ictum totis corporibus expositi numquam frustra manum mittunt. Non galea, non scuto repellitur ferrum. 'Sed latrocinium fecit aliquis.' Quid ergo? occidit hominem? 'Occidit hominem.' Quia occidit,
10 ille meruit ut hoc pateretur: tu quid meruisti, miser, ut hoc spectes? 'Occide, verbera, ure! Quare tam timide incurrit in ferrum? Quare parum libenter moritur et plagis agitur in vulnera? Intermissum est spectaculum: interim iugulentur homines, ne nihil agatur.'

SENECA, *Ep.* 7

l. 1   *meridianum spectaculum:* literally 'the midday games, i.e. 'the games at midday'. At such shows (*spectacula*), the morning was usually devoted to wild beast hunts, the afternoon to gladiatorial combats. At midday there was a lunch break, often filled by some light entertainment, but on this occasion Seneca found condemned criminals being forced to fight each other.

l. 2   *sales:* 'wit, fun'   *aliquid laxamenti:* 'some relaxation'.

l. 3   *cruor:* 'bloodshed'.

l. 4   *quidquid ante pugnatum est:* 'all the previous fighting'.

l. 5   *omissis nugis:* literally 'trifling omitted' i.e. 'in real earnest'.

l. 6   *ictus, ictus:* 'a blow' *numquam frustra manum mittunt:* 'they never strike in vain'.

l. 7   *galea:* 'a helmet'.

l. 8   '*Sed latrocinium . . .*': the passages in inverted commas are spoken by an imaginary spectator.

l. 11   *verberare:* 'to beat'.

l. 13   *plaga:* 'a blow'.

l. 14   *iugulare:* 'to murder'.

1. What did Seneca expect to find when he dropped in to the show?
2. What did he in fact find?
3. How did the fights he saw differ from ordinary gladiatorial combats?
4. How does Seneca's imaginary spectator attempt to defend what is going on?
5. What does Seneca mean by *tu quid . . . spectes* (ll. 10–11)? Account for the position of *tu*.
6. How do the real feelings of the imaginary spectator emerge?
7. Explain the meaning of the last sentence *Intermissum est . . . agatur*. Why does Seneca make his spectator say this?
8. Summarize Seneca's attitude to such games and to the crowd which enjoys them.

(i) In what case is each of the following words, and why: *lusus* (l. 1); *laxamenti* (l. 2); *galea* (l. 7)?

(ii) *quo tegantur* (ll. 5–6); *iugulentur* (l. 14): translate the phrases in which these verbs occur so that the meaning of the subjunctive is clear in each case.

ii. An advertisement from Pompeii

This advertisement is boldly and elaborately painted on a wall in Pompeii; the sign writer gives his name in the last line.

D. Lucreti Satri Valentis flaminis Neronis Caesaris Augusti fili perpetui gladiatorum paria XX et D. Lucreti Valentis fili gladiatorum paria X pugnabunt Pompeis VI, V, IV, III, pridie Idus Apriles. Venatio
5 legitima et vela erunt.
  Scripsit Aemilius Celer singulus ad lunam.

Dessau 5145

iii. Caesar's triumphal games

After his final victory in the Civil Wars Julius Caesar gave entertainments on an unprecedented scale.

Edidit spectacula varii generis: munus gladiatorium, ludos, item circenses, athletas, naumachiam. Venationes editae per dies quinque ac novissime pugna divisa est in duas acies, quingenis peditibus, elephantis vicenis,
5 tricenis equitibus hinc et inde commissis. Navali proelio in minore Codeta defosso lacu biremes ac triremes quadriremesque Tyriae et Aegyptiae classis magno pugnatorum numero conflixerunt. Ad quae omnia spectacula tantum undique confluxit hominum, ut
10 plerique advenae aut inter vicos aut inter vias tabernaculis positis manerent, ac saepe prae turba elisi exanimatique sint plurimi et in his duo senatores.

SUETONIUS, *Divus Julius* 39

1. List the different kinds of entertainment given by Caesar.
2. What details are given about (*a*) the fight on the last day, (*b*) the naval battle?
3. What evidence is there that these entertainments were popular?

D. Lucreti . . . perpetui: the name and title of the donor is given in the genitive case, which depends on *paria* ('pairs . . . belonging to . . .'); he was *flamen perpetuus*, 'priest for life', of the local cult of the emperor (*Nero Caesar Augusti filius*).

l. 4   *venatio:* 'hunting', i.e. wild beast hunts in the arena.
l. 5   *legitimus:* 'regular', i.e. full scale   *vela:* 'awnings' to keep the sun off the spectators.
l. 6   *singulus ad lunam* appears to mean 'alone by moonlight'; the streets were presumably too crowded for him to work by day.

1. Who, according to this advertisement, will be giving the show?
2. How many gladiators will fight altogether?
3. On what dates will the show take place?
4. What other entertainment will there be?

l. 2   *ludos:* 'stage plays'.
l. 3   *item circenses, athletas, naumachiam:* 'also chariot races, athletic competitions and a mock sea battle'.
l. 4   *novissime:* 'last of all'.
ll. 5–6   *quingenis . . . vicensis . . . tricenis . . . hinc et inde:* '500 . . . 20 . . . 30 . . . on each side'.
l. 7   *in mimore Codeta:* a marshy district on the Campus Martius, by the Tiber.   *defodere:* 'to dig out'.
ll. 7–8   *biremes, triremes, quadriremes:* ships with respectively two, three and four banks of oars.
l. 10   *tantum . . . hominum:* literally 'so much of men', i.e. 'such crowds'.
l. 11   *advena -ae:* 'a stranger, a visitor'.   *vicus -i:* 'a street'. *tabernaculum:* 'a tent'.
l. 12   *elisi exanimatique:* 'crushed and killed'.

iv. Riot at Pompeii

Sub idem tempus levi initio atrox caedes orta est inter
colonos Nucerinos Pompeianosque gladiatorio spectaculo quod Liveneius Regulus edebat. Quippe oppidana
lascivia in vicem incessentes probra, dein saxa, postremo
5 ferrum sumpsere, validiore Pompeianorum plebe, apud
quos spectaculum edebatur. Ergo deportati sunt in
urbem multi e Nucerinis trunco per vulnera corpore, ac
plerique liberorum aut parentum mortes deflebant.
Cuius rei iudicium princeps senatui, senatus consulibus
10 permisit. Et rursus re ad patres relata, prohibiti publice
in decem annos eius modi coetu Pompeiani, collegiaque,
quae contra leges instituerant, dissoluta; Liveneius et qui
alii seditionem conciverant exilio multati sunt.

TACITUS, *Annals* xiv, 17

l. 2   *colonos Nucerinos:* 'the inhabitants of Nuceria'; Nuceria was near Pompeii. The inhabitants are called *coloni* because the town had the rank of a Roman settlement (*colonia*).

ll. 3–4   *Quippe oppidana lascivia:* 'for, with the wildness common in country towns, . . .'   *in vicem:* literally 'in turn', i.e. 'at each other'   *probrum:* 'an insult'   *incessere:* 'to throw'.

l. 7   *truncus:* 'maimed'.

l. 9   *princeps:* 'the emperor'.

l. 11   *coetus -us:* 'gathering'   *collegia,* n.pl.: 'clubs, unions'.

l. 13   *seditio:* 'rebellion, riot'   *multare:* 'to punish'.

1. On what occasion did the riot take place and where? Who were involved?

2. By what stages did it develop?

3. Who came off best? (Quote the words which show you.)

4. *urbem* (l. 7): what city is meant? Why is *deportati sunt* more suitable to the context than e.g. *ierunt*? Why did the Nucerini go there?

5. What procedure did the enquiry follow, and before whom were the offenders eventually tried?

6. How were the Pompeians punished (two punishments)?

7. How was Liveneius punished? Why was he given special treatment?

8. Explain with reference to the Latin what is meant by *levi initio atrox caedes orta est* (l. 1).

9. What light does the passage throw on the following scribble found on a wall of Pompeii: *Puteolanis feliciter, Nucerinis felicia, et uncum Pompeianis* (Puteoli is another town in the district; *uncum* = 'death to')?

10. What would be the nearest parallel in modern life to the events here described?

(i) On which word does *liberorum aut parentum* (l. 8) depend?

(ii) Distinguish the following uses of the ablative: *levi initio* (l. 1); *gladiatorio spectaculo* (ll. 2–3); *validiore plebe* (l. 5)

53

10. The Races

i. An epitaph on a charioteer

Dis manibibus Epaphroditus, agitator factionis rus-
satae. Vicit clxxviii, et apud purpuream vicit viii. Beia
Feicula fecit coniugi suo bene merenti.

Dessau 5282

Say all you can on Epaphroditus on the evidence of this
inscription.

ii. Ovid at the races 1

Non ego nobilium sedeo studiosus equorum;
    cui tamen ipsa faves, vincat ut ille, precor.
ut loquerer tecum, veni, tecumque sederem,
    ne tibi non notus, quem facis, esset amor.
5 tu cursus spectas, ego te: spectemus uterque
    quod iuvat atque oculos pascat uterque suos.
o, cuicumque faves, felix agitator equorum!
    ergo illi curae contigit esse tuae?
hoc mihi contingat, sacro de carcere missis
10   insistam forti mente vehendus equis
et modo lora dabo, modo verbere terga notabo,
    nunc stringam metas interiore rota;
si mihi currenti fueris conspecta, morabor,
    deque meis manibus lora remissa fluent.

OVID, Amores III, ii, 1–14

factio russata: 'the red team'; the other teams were *prasina* (green), *veneta* (blue), *alba* (white). The emperor Domitian added *purpurea* and *aurata* but these extra teams were probably running only in his reign (A.D. 81–96).

l. 1   *studiosus* + gen. : 'keen on'.
l. 2   The word order in prose might be: *precor tamen ut ille vincat cui ipsa faves*.
l. 6   *pascere:* 'to feed, feast'.
l. 8   *illi contigit:* 'it has happened to him' (usually of good luck) *curae esse tuae:* 'to be your care' (predicative dative), i.e. 'to be cared for by you'.
l. 9   *hoc mihi contingat . . . :* 'were this to be my luck . . .'   *carcer:* 'the starting gate'   *insistere* + dative: 'to urge on'.
l. 10   *vehi:* 'to be carried, to drive';   *vehendus* (gerundive) is here used as a present passive participle 'driving'.
l. 11   *lora* (n.pl.) : 'the reins'.
l. 12   *meta -ae* 'the turning post'   *stringere:* 'to graze'.
l. 13   *mihi:* 'by me' (= *a me*).
l. 14   *remissus:* 'slack'.

1. Where is Ovid sitting?
2. What would be the modern English term for *nobilium* (l. 1)?
3. Why has Ovid come to the races?
4. What does Ovid watch? What is the significance of the change of mood from *spectas* to *spectemus* (l. 5)?
5. Which charioteer is described as *felix* (l. 7)? Why is he *felix?*
6. What does Ovid imagine in lines 9–11?
7. Draw a picture of what is described in line 12.
8. What does *currenti* (l. 13) here mean?
9. Why does Ovid say he will go slow? What will happen to the reins?
10. What is the mood of this passage? How serious is Ovid being?

Maxima iam vacuo praetor spectacula Circo
    quadriiugos aequo carcere misit equos.
cui studeas, video; vincet, cuicumque favebis;
    quid cupias, ipsi scire videntur equi.
5 me miserum, metam spatioso circuit orbe;
    quid facis? admoto proximus axe subit.
quid facis, infelix? perdis bona vota puellae;
    tende, precor, valida lora sinistra manu.
favimus ignavo. sed enim revocate, Quirites,
10   et date iactatis undique signa togis.
en revocant; at, ne turbet toga mota capillos,
    in nostros abdas te licet usque sinus.
iamque patent iterum reserato carcere postes,
    evolat admissis discolor agmen equis.
15 nunc saltem supera spatioque insurge patenti:
    sint mea, sint dominae fac rata vota meae.
sunt dominae rata vota meae, mea vota supersunt;
    ille tenet palmam, palma petenda mea est.'
risit, et argutis quiddam promisit ocellis;
20   'hoc satis hic; alio cetera redde loco.'

OVID, *Amores* III, ii, 65–end

l. 1   *vacuo . . .* Circo: Ovid has just described the procession which preceded the actual races; the latter are called *maxima spectacula.*

l. 5   *circuit:* 'he is rounding'.

l. 6   *subire:* 'to come close, come up to'   *axis:* 'axle'.

l. 7   *votum:* 'a prayer, wish'.

l. 11   *en:* 'look!'   *capilli -orum:* 'hair'.

l. 12   *sinus -us:* 'fold' (of a toga).

l. 13   *reserare:* 'to unfasten'.

l. 14   *admittere:* 'to let go'.

l. 15   *saltem:* 'at least'   *insurgere:* 'to rise up, to gallop'.

l. 16   *fac:* imperative of *facio,* 'see that', here followed directly by the subjunctive: *fac mea vota rata sint:* 'see that my prayers be fulfilled'.

l. 19   *argutus:* 'bright, lively'.

1. What has the *praetor* done (ll. 1–2)? What do you suppose *aequo* means in this context? What was a *praetor* and what was he doing at the games?

2. What sort of start does the team backed by Ovid's girl make?

3. *me miserum* (l. 5): why is this case used? What has upset Ovid?

4. *quid facis* (l. 6): whom is Ovid addressing here? Why do you suppose Ovid has changed the grammatical person?

5. *tende . . . manu* (l. 8): in this line, which adjectives agree with which nouns? How do you know? Why does Ovid tell him to do this?

6. *favimus ignavo* (l. 9): why is the charioteer called *ignavus*? What significance do you see in the grammatical person used here?

7. Who are addressed as *Quirites* (l. 9)? What signal was given when the crowd demanded a re-start? Under what circumstances do you suppose a re-start was allowed?

8. Lines 11–12: to whom is Ovid speaking here? What does he suggest that he, or she, should do, and why?

9. Lines 13–14: if you had been sitting beside Ovid, what would you have seen happening in the Circus at this point?

10. What does Ovid mean by *palma petenda mea est* (l. 18)?

11. Lines 19–20: Who smiled? Explain *hoc satis hic.*

iv. Pliny not at the races

Omne hoc tempus inter pugillares ac libellos incundis-
sima quiete transmisi. 'Quemadmodum' inquis 'in urbe
potuisti?' Circenses erant, quo genere spectaculi ne
levissime quidem teneor. Nihil novum, nihil varium,
5 nihil quod non semel spectasse sufficiat. Quo magis
miror tot milia virorum tam pueriliter identidem cupere
currentes equos, insistentes curribus homines videre. Si
tamen aut velocitate equorum aut hominum arte traherentur, esset ratio non nulla; nunc favent panno,
10 pannum amant, et, si in ipso cursu medioque certamine
hic color illuc ille huc transferatur, studium favorque
transibit. Tanta gratia, tanta auctoritas in una vilissima
tunica, non modo apud vulgus, quod vilius est tunica,
sed apud quosdam graves homines; quos ego cum
15 recordor in re inani tam insatiabiliter desidere, capio
aliquam voluptatem, quod hac voluptate non capior.
Ac per hos dies libentissime otium meum in litteris
colloco, quos alii otiosissimis occupationibus perdunt.
Vale.

PLINY, *Ep*. IX, vi

(i) l. 5 *nihil . . . sufficiat:* translate, so that the meaning of
the subjunctive is clear.

(ii) ll. 7–9 *Si traherentur, esset ratio:* translate, so that the
meaning of the subjunctive is clear.

(iii) *quos* (l. 14): to whom does this refer and why is it in
this case?

l. 1   *pugillares:* 'writing tablets, note books'.

l. 3   *Cirenses* supply *ludi*.

l. 4   *tenere:* 'to hold, attract'.

l. 5   *spectasse = spectavisse*   *sufficit:* 'it is enough'   *quo magis miror:* 'and so I am all the more surprised'.

l. 6   *identidem:* 'again and again'.

l. 8   *trahere:* 'to draw'.

l. 10   *pannus:* 'cloth, racing colours'.

l. 12   *gratia:* 'influence'.

l. 13   *vilis:* 'cheap, worthless'.

l. 15   *inanis* -e: 'empty, useless'.

l. 15   *desidere:* 'to sit idle'.

l. 18   *perdere:* 'to waste'.

1. Where has Pliny been staying?
2. What has he been doing?
3. What does the question '*Quemadmodum in urbe potuisti?*' (ll. 2–3) imply about life in the city?
4. How has it been possible for him to spend his time *iucundissima quiete* (ll. 1–2)?
5. How did Pliny feel about the games and why did he feel like this (ll. 4–5)?
6. What surprises Pliny? Which phrases in this sentence indicate his contempt for the whole business?
7. What, according to Pliny, would be a reasonable motive for going to the races?
8. Why, according to Pliny, do the crowd go? Why do you suppose the word *pannus* is repeated (l. 10), and why is this word order used?
9. Paraphrase in English *et, si* (l. 10) . . . *transibit* (l. 12).
10. Explain the meaning of *Tanta gratia . . . tunica* (ll. 12–13).
11. What does *graves* (l. 14) mean here? Are these people behaving like *graves*?
12. What two meanings of *otium* are suggested by the last sentence?
13. Summarize Pliny's reasons for despising the crowd. If his remarks are true, why do you imagine the crowd went to the races? How far would the remarks apply to a crowd at a race meeting to-day?
14. Which two passages in the letter give clearest evidence of Pliny's complacency?

11. Hunting

i. Dido and Aeneas go hunting

Oceanum interea surgens Aurora reliquit.
it portis iubare exorto delecta iuventus,
retia rara, plagae, lato venabula ferro,
Massylique ruunt equites et odora canum vis.
5 reginam thalamo cunctantem ad limina primi
Poenorum exspectant, ostroque insignis et auro
stat sonipes ac frena ferox spumantia mandit.
tandem progreditur magna stipante caterva . . .
nec non et Phrygii comites et laetus Iulus
10 incedunt. ipse ante alios pulcherrimus omnes
infert se socium Aeneas atque agmina iungit . . .
postquam altos ventum in montes atque invia lustra,
ecce ferae saxi deiectae vertice caprae
decurrere iugis; alia de parte patentes
15 transmittunt cursu campos atque agmina cervi
pulverulenta fuga glomerant montesque relinquunt.
at puer Ascanius mediis in vallibus acri
gaudet equo iamque hos cursu, iam praeterit illos,
spumantemque dari pecora inter inertia votis
20 optat aprum, aut fulvum descendere monte leonem.

VIRGIL, *Aeneid* iv, 129–59 (with omissions)

l. 1   *Aurora:* 'Dawn'.

l. 2   *iubar, iubaris:* 'sun beam'   *delectus:* 'chosen, choice'.

l. 3   *retia rara:* 'wide-meshed nets' (for surrounding coverts) *plagae:* 'trap-nets'   *lato venabula ferro:* 'hunting spears with broad blade'.

l. 4   *Massyli:* 'Massylian' i.e. African   *odora canum vis:* literally 'the keen-scented strength of dogs' i.e. strong, keen-scented hounds'.

l. 5   *thalamo:* 'in her room'   *ad limina:* 'at the door'.

l. 6   *ostrum:* 'purple'.

l. 7   *sonipes:* 'a horse'   *frena,* n.pl: 'bit'   *spumare:* 'to foam'.

l. 8   *stipare:* 'to press, throng round'.

l. 9   *Phrygii:* 'the Trojans'   *Iulus:* Aeneas' son, also called Ascanius (l. 17).

l. 11   *infert se socium:* literally 'brings himself as her companion' i.e. 'comes to join her'.

l. 12   *ventum:* supply *est;* 'it was come' = 'they came'.

l. 13   *deiectae* 'thrown down, driven down' (by the beaters) *vertex, verticis:* 'the top'   *capra:* 'a goat'.

l. 14   *iugum:* 'mountain pass, mountain'.

l. 15   *cervus:* 'a deer'.

l. 16   *pulverulentus:* 'dusty'   *glomerare:* 'to join, unite'.

l. 19   *pecora inertia:* 'the harmless beats'.

l. 20   *optare:* 'to pray, wish, long for'   *aper, apri:* 'a boar'.

1. Where, and at what time of day, did the hunt gather?

2. Who took part in the hunt? (see ll. 2–11).

3. What equipment was used? After reading the whole passage, suggest how it would have been used.

4. Describe Dido's horse. Why does Virgil call it a *sonipes* (l. 7)?

5. Where did the hunters find their game? What game did they find? How did each sort of game behave when it was found?

6. How does the rhythm of line 16 help to express the sense?

7. How does Ascanius behave? What are his feelings, and what does he pray for, and why?

8. What impression of the hunt do you form from this description? Which Latin phrases particularly contribute to your impression?

ii. Pliny goes hunting

C. Plinius Cornelio Tacito suo s.

Ridebis, et licet rideas. Ego ille, quem nosti, apros tres
et pulcherrimos cepi. 'Ipse?' inquis. Ipse; non tamen ut
omnino ab inertia mea et quiete discederem. Ad retia
sedebam; erat in proximo non venabulum aut lancea,
5 sed stilus et pugillares; meditabar aliquid enotabamque,
ut si manus vacuas, plenas tamen ceras reportarem.
Non est quod contemnas hoc studendi genus; mirum est
ut animus agitatione corporis excitetur; iam undique
silvae et solitudo ipsumque illud silentium quod vena-
10 tioni datur, magna cogitationis incitamenta sunt.
Proinde cum venabere, licebit auctore me, ut panarium
et lagunculam, sic etiam pugillares feras: experieris non
Dianam magis in montibus quam Minervam inerrare.
Vale.

PLINY, *Ep.*, i, 6

iii. A hunter's vow fulfilled

Silvano invicto sacrum. C. Tettius Veturius Micianus,
praef. alae Sebosianae, ob aprum eximiae formae
captum, quem multi antecessores eius praedari non
potuerunt, voto soluto libens posuit.

Inscription on an altar found at Stanhope,
near Lancaster.

l. 2 *praef.* = *praefectus* 'commander'.
l. 2 *alae Sebosianae:* an auxiliary cavalry wing, raised in Gaul and
serving in Britain.
l. 2 *eximius:* 'outstanding'.
l. 3 *praedari:* 'to catch'.
l. 4 *votum:* 'a vow'.

l. 1   Pliny is writing to Cornelius Tacitus, the historian
nosti = novisti.

l. 3   *inertia:* 'inactivity, laziness'.

l. 3   *ad retia:* 'by the nets'   *venabulum:* 'thrusting spear'.

l. 4   *lancea:* 'throwing spear'   *stilus:* a pointed bronze instrument for writing on wax tablets   *meditari:* 'to think, to compose'.

l. 6   *cera:* 'wax, a wax tablet'.

l. 7   *non est quod:* 'there is no reason why'.

ll. 7–8   *mirum est ut:* 'it is wonderful how'.

l. 10   *incitamenta*, (n.pl.): 'stimulants'   *proinde:* 'and so'.

l. 11   *panarium:* 'bread basket, picnic basket'   *laguncula:* 'flask'.

l. 12   *experiri:* 'to find (by experience)'.

(i) Distinguish the following uses of *ut: ut . . . discederem* (l. 3); *ut . . . reportarem* (l. 6); *ut . . . lagunculam* (l. 12).

(ii) Parse *venabere* (l. 11).

(iii) Explain the case and meaning of *auctore me* (l. 12).

1. What is the main piece of news Pliny is giving Tacitus? How does he expect Tacitus to react to it (there are three clues to this in the first two lines)?

2. *inertia* (l. 3): does Pliny really expect Tacitus to think of him as *iners?*

3. What did Pliny do as he waited? Why did he do this? Suggest why Pliny uses the word-order *manus vacuas, plenas tamen ceras* (l. 6).

4. Pliny gives two reasons why *hoc studendi genus* (l. 7) should not be despised. What are they? Do you find them both convincing?

5. What does Pliny advise Tacitus to do when hunting?

6. Explain what Pliny means by *experieris . . . inerrare* (ll. 12–13).

7. Give a brief account of the sort of hunting here described, basing your account on the contents of the letter.

8. What is the tone of the letter as a whole i.e. what are Pliny's feelings about his exploit and how does he wish to represent it to Tacitus? If you find the tone changes in places, explain where and in what way.

1. Why did Veturius dedicate this altar?

2. To whom did he dedicate it? Judging from the root of the word, what sort of deity was this?

3. What light does the inscription throw on the flora and fauna of Lancashire in the period of Roman occupation?

12. Ships and the sea-side

i. Sailing from Greece to Italy

Cicero has returned from Cilicia, where he was governor, to Italy. He writes to his secretary, Tiro (a freedman), whom he has left in Greece suffering from a stomach disorder.

Nos eo die cenati solvimus. Inde austro lenissimo, caelo sereno, nocte illa et die postero in Italiam ad Hydruntem ludibundi pervenimus; eodem vento postridie—id erat a.d. VII Kal. Dec.—hora quarta
5 Brundisium venimus. A. D. V Kal. Dec. servus Cn. Plancii Brundisii tandem aliquando mihi a te exspectatissimas litteras reddidit, datas Idibus Novembribus, quae me molestia valde levaverunt: utinam omnino liberavissent! sed tamen Asclapo medicus plane con-
10 firmat propediem te valentem fore.

Nunc quid ego te horter ut omnem diligentiam adhibeas ad convalescendum? Tuam prudentiam, temperantiam, amorem erga me novi: scio te omnia facturum ut nobiscum quam primum sis: sed tamen ita
15 velim, ut ne quid properes. Reliquum est ut te hoc rogem et a te petam, ne temere naviges—solent nautae festinare quaestus sui causa; cautus sis, mi Tiro—mare magnum et difficile tibi restat. Etiam atque etiam, noster Tiro, vale. Medico de te scripsi diligentissime. Vale et salve.

CICERO, *ad Fam.*, xvi, 9

l. 1   *solvimus = navem solvimus*   *auster:* 'the south wind'.

l. 3   *Hydrus, Hydruntis:* a town on the heel of Italy (modern Otranto)   *ludibundus:* literally 'playing' i.e. the voyage was child's play.

l. 4   *a. d. VII Kal. Dec. = ante diem septimum Kalendas Decembres* i.e. 26 November.

l. 7   *Idibus =* 13 November.

l. 8   *molestia:* 'worry'   *levare:* 'to lighten, to relieve'.

l. 10   *propediem:* 'soon'.

· l. 11   *adhibere:* 'to use'   *quid:* 'why?'

l. 16   *temere:* 'rashly'   *quaestus -us:* 'gain, profit'.

l. 18   *restare:* 'to remain, await'.

1. On what date and at what time of day did Cicero set sail? Considering they had no compass and few navigation lights, what strikes you about the time of sailing?
2. What conditions did he have for his voyage?
3. On what date and at what time did he arrive at Brindisi? How long did the voyage from Greece to Brindisi take?
4. How long did the letter from Tiro take to reach Cicero? How was it delivered? What evidence is there that Cicero felt it had taken a good deal too long?
5. What news did the letter bring? Was the news as good as Cicero could have wished?
6. In lines 12–15 Cicero has conflicting feelings about the situation. Explain what they are.
7. What worries Cicero about Tiro's prospective voyage?
8. Explain the point of *solent nautae festinare quaestus sui causa* (ll. 16–17).
9. What does the letter show you about relations between Cicero and Tiro?
10. What can you learn from the letter about conditions of travel and communication in Cicero's day?

(i) Distinguish the following uses of the subjunctive: *liberavisset* (l. 9); *horter* (l. 11); *velim* (l. 15); *sis* (l. 17).

(ii) *datas* (l. 7): with which word does this agree? Explain what it means. What English word is derived from this usage.

(iii) What is the function of *hoc* (l. 15)?

6   65

ii. A rough passage

Seneca Lucilio suo salutem

Quid non potest mihi persuaderi, cui persuasum est
ut navigarem? Solvi mari languido. Erat sine dubio
caelum grave sordidis nubibus, sed putavi tam pauca
milia a Parthenope tua usque Puteolos surripi posse,
5 quamvis dubio et impendente caelo. Itaque quo celerius
evaderem, protinus per altum ad Nesida derexi prae-
cisurus omnes sinus. Cum iam eo processissem ut mea
nihil interesset utrum irem an redirem, primum aequa-
litas illa, quae me corruperat, periit. Nondum erat
10 tempestas, sed iam inclinatio maris ac subinde crebrior
fluctus. Coepi gubernatorem rogare ut me in aliquo
litore exponeret. Aiebat ille aspera esse litora et impor-
tuosa nec quicquam se aeque in tempestate timere quam
terram. Peius autem vexabar quam ut mihi periculum
15 succurreret. Nausea enim me segnis haec et sine exitu
torquebat, quae bilem movet nec effundit. Institi itaque
gubernatori et illum, vellet nollet, coegi petere litus.

SENECA *Ep.*, 53

l. 2   *solvi = navem solvi*   *languidus:* 'sluggish'.

l. 4   *Parthenope:* Naples   *Puteoli:* Pozzuoli, about ten miles west of Naples   *surripere:* 'to snatch, to steal'.

l. 5   *quamvis:* 'however much, however'   *impendere:* 'to threaten'.

l. 6   *protinus* (adv.): 'straight'   *derigere:* 'to steer'   *praecidere:* 'to cut off'.

l. 7   *sinus -us:* 'fold, bay'.

ll. 7–8   *mea nihil interest:* 'it makes no difference to me'.

l. 9   *corrumpere:* 'to deceive'.

l. 10   *subinde:* 'continually'   *creber:* 'frequent'.

l. 12   *importuosus:* 'harbourless'.

ll. 14–15   *Peius ... succurreret:* literally 'I was worse troubled than that danger should occur to me' i.e. 'I was in too bad a way to think of danger'.

l. 15   *segnis:* 'slack, slow'.

l. 17   *instare:* 'to press'.

1. Express the meaning of the first sentence in natural English. What is the implication of the question?
2. Describe what the weather was like when Seneca sailed.
3. Explain the meaning of *putavi ... caelo* (ll. 3–5). Why is *surripi* an appropriate word in the context?
4. Why did Seneca sail *protinus per altum* (l. 6)? What else might he have done?
5. At what stage of the voyage did the calm cease?
6. How did the sea then behave?
7. What did Seneca then ask the helmsman to do?
8. What was the helmsman's reply? Was he showing good sense?
9. Why was Seneca in such a bad way? Describe his symptoms as exactly as possible.
10. In this predicament, what did Seneca do? Was such conduct worthy of a professed Stoic?

(i) Explain the grammar and meaning of *quid ... persuaderi* (l. 1).

(ii) *mari languido* (l. 2): in what case is this phrase and why?

(iii) *quo celerius evaderem* (ll. 5–6): why is the subjunctive used here?

(iv) What is the meaning and function of *eo* (l. 7)?

(v) *vellet nollet* (l. 17): what does this mean? What English expression is similar to this phrase?

iii. The perils of the sea-side

Propertius addresses this poem to Cynthia; she is on holiday at Baiae, while he remains in Rome. Baiae was a popular sea-side resort on the bay of Naples. A few miles east of Baiae lay the Lucrine lake, separated from the sea by a narrow causeway, legendarily supposed to have been built by Hercules (see ll. 2 and 8).

Ecquid te mediis cessantem, Cynthia, Bais,
    qua iacet Herculeis semita litoribus,
nostri cura subit memores adducere noctes?
    ecquis in extremo restat amore locus?
5 an te nescioquis simulatis ignibus hostis
    sustulit e nostris, Cynthia, carminibus?
atque utinam mage te remis confisa minutis
    parvula Lucrina cumba moretur aqua,
aut teneat clausam tenui Teuthrantis in unda
10   alternae facilis cedere lympha manu,
quam vacet alterius blandos audire susurros
    molliter in tacito litore compositam!
tu mihi sola domus, tu, Cynthia, sola parentes,
    omnia tu nostrae tempora laetitiae.
15 seu tristis veniam seu contra laetus amicis,
    quidquid ero, dicam 'Cynthia causa fuit.'
tu modo quam primum corruptas desere Baias:
    multis ista dabunt litora discidium,
litora quae fuerunt castis inimica puellis:
20   a pereant Baiae, crimen amoris, aquae!

PROPERTIUS i, 11

ll. 1 and 3 literally: 'Does any care for me come over you, Cynthia, as you linger in the midst of Baiae, to bring (you) nights that remember (me)?'

l. 1 *ecquid* (adv.): introduces a question.

l. 2 *semita:* 'path, causeway'   *nostri = mei* (compare *nostrae = meae* l. 14).

l. 3 *adducere:* the infinitive is here used to express consequence.

l. 4 *ecquis locus:* 'does any place . . . ?'

l. 5 *nesciosquis . . . hostis:* 'some enemy or other'.

ll. 7–11   the structure is: *utinam mage te . . . cumba moretur . . . aut lympha teneat (te) clausam . . ., quam vacet . . .*: 'rather may a boat keep you . . . or the water hold you shut . . ., than that you should have time . . .'   *cumba:* a rowing boat.

l. 7   *mage = magis   remis minutis:* 'tiny oars'.

l. 9   Teuthras was the name of another small lake.

l. 10   'water easily yielding to alternate hands': *manu = manui; facilis cedere:* 'easy to yield' = 'easily yielding'.

l. 11   *quam vacet (te):* 'than that you should have time . . .' *blandus:* 'winning, tempting'   *susurrus:* 'whisper'.

l. 12   *compositus:* 'lying'.

l. 15   *contra* (adv.): 'on the other hand'.

l. 18   *discidium:* 'parting, separation'.

l. 19   *castus:* 'faithful'.

l. 20   *crimen amoris:* 'reproach to love'   *a:* 'ah!' (exclamatory).

1. What is Propertius' worry in lines 1–6?
2. What is meant by *in extremo amore* (l. 4)?
3. Explain in detail lines 5–6. In line 6 a stage in thought seems to be left out; what is it?
4. In lines 7–10, what does he hope Cynthia is doing?
5. In lines 11–12, what does he hope she is not doing?
6. With which words do *confisa* (l. 7), *parvula* and *Lucrina* (l. 8) agree? How do you know?
7. What does he mean in ordinary language by lines 13–16?
8. Lines 17–18: what does he tell Cynthia to do? and why?
9. Why are the waters of Baiae called *crimen amoris* (l. 20)?
10. Which parts of this poem seem to you most clearly visualised? Explain what you mean.
11. Write a letter to a girl on holiday in Brighton, following the same sequence of ideas as Propertius.

13. Four girls

i. An incomparable girl

Salve, nec minimo puella naso
nec bello pede nec nigris ocellis
nec longis digitis nec ore sicco
nec sane nimis elegante lingua,
decoctoris amica Formiani.
ten provincia narrat esse bellam?
tecum Lesbia nostra comparatur?
o saeclum insapiens et infacetum!

CATULLUS 43

ii. A faithless girl

Nulli se dicit mulier mea nubere malle
quam mihi, non si se Iuppiter ipse petat.
dicit: sed mulier cupido quod dicit amanti
in vento et rapida scribere oportet aqua.

CATULLUS 70

l. 1 *salve:* 'greetings' *nasus:* 'nose'.
l. 2 *bellus:* 'pretty'.
l. 3 *siccus:* 'dry'.
l. 4 *nec sane:* 'nor indeed'.
l. 5 *decoctor Formianus:* 'the bankrupt from Formiae'. **Mamurra,** a man Catullus intensely disliked, lived at Formiae.
l. 6 *ten = tene?* *provincia:* this refers to the province of Cisalpine Gaul (North Italy), where Catullus' home was.
l. 8 *saeclum:* 'age, generation' *infacetus:* 'tasteless'.

1. On the evidence of lines 1–3, describe Mamurra's *amica.*
2. *lingua* (l. 4) : this is unlikely to refer to physical appearance; why? What meanings could the line have?
3. In lines 6 and 7, what is the effect of the repeated *te?* How can Latin here achieve an effect which is impossible in natural English?
4. How would this poem have been received by (a) Mamurra (b) Catullus' fellow countrymen (c) Lesbia?
5. Scan lines 1 and 2. In what metre is the poem written? How does the rhythmical structure of the poem help to express its feeling? (To answer this, read the poem aloud again and consider how the punctuation and the length of the words has the effect of slowing down or speeding up the rhythm.)

l. 3 *mulier ... amanti:* 'what a woman says ...' *cupidus:* 'eager'.

1. What does Lesbia say to Catullus?
2. What is his comment on what she says?
3. What is the feeling of the poem?
4. Compare the last two lines to the following:

> Woman's faith and woman's trust—
> Write the characters in dust,
> Stamp them on the running stream,
> Print them on the moonlight's beam.
>
> (WALTER SCOTT, *The Betrothed*)

Which seems to you the stronger statement of the lover's predicament? Which seems to you more 'poetic'? What do you mean by 'poetic'?

iii. A shocking girl

Sallust has given a list of the men who took part in Catiline's revolutionary conspiracy; he goes on to say that there were some women in it too.

Sed in eis erat Sempronia, quae multa saepe virilis audaciae facinora commiserat. Haec mulier genere atque forma, praeterea viro, liberis satis fortunata fuit; litteris Graecis et Latinis docta, psallere, saltare elegan-
5 tius quam necesse est probae, multa alia quae instrumenta luxuriae sunt. Sed ei cariora semper omnia quam decus atque pudicitia fuerunt; pecuniae an famae minus parceret, haud facile discerneres. Sed ea saepe antehac fidem prodiderat, creditum abiuraverat, caedis conscia
10 fuerat, luxuria atque inopia praeceps abierat. Verum ingenium eius haud absurdum: posse versus facere, iocum movere, sermone uti vel modesto vel molli vel procaci; prorsus multae facetiae multusque lepos inerat.

SALLUST, *Catiline* 25

l. 3   *forma:* 'beauty'   *viro, liberis:* after *viro,* supply 'and'.

l. 4   *litteris:* 'literature'   *psallere:* 'she played the *cithara*' (an instrument not unlike the guitar).

l. 4   *saltare:* 'she danced': historic infinitives   *probus:* 'good'.

ll. 5–6   *instrumenta luxuriae:* 'means to indulgence'.

l. 7   *pecuniae an famae:* before *pecuniae,* supply *utrum*   *haud facile discerneres:* 'you could not easily have told'.

l. 9   *creditum abiuraverat:* 'she had foresworn a trust' i.e. she had kept money etc. entrusted to her.

l. 11   *verum:* 'but'   *haud absurdum:* 'not despicable'.

l. 11   *posse:* historic infinitive.

l. 13   *procax:* 'shameless'   *prorsus* (adv.): 'in fact'.

l. 13   *lepos:* 'charm'.

1. What is meant by *virilis audaciae facinora* (l. 2) ?
2. In what respects was Sempronia lucky?
3. What accomplishments did she have (ll. 4–5) ? What fault does Sallust find with these accomplishments?
4. Translate *Sed ei semper . . . discerneres* (ll. 6–8) into appropriate English. Summarize in three words in English the faults here ascribed to her.
5. What crimes had she committed? Explain the meaning of *luxuria . . . abierat* (l. 10).
6. What redeeming features had she?
7. Read the passage again. Write a description of Sempronia's character in English without looking at the Latin.
8. What seems to you to be Sallust's attitude to Sempronia?

73

iv. A birthday girl

Mirabar quidnam visissent mane Camenae
    ante meum stantes sole rubente torum.
natalis nostrae signum misere puellae
    et manibus faustos ter crepuere sonos.
5 transeat hic sine nube dies, stent aëre venti,
    ponat et in sicco molliter unda minas.
aspiciam nullos hodierna luce dolentes,
    et Niobae lacrimas supprimat ipse lapis.
tuque, o cara mihi, felicibus edita pennis,
10   surge et poscentes iusta precare deos.
ac primum pura somnum tibi discute lympha,
    et nitidas presso pollice finge comas:
dein qua primum oculos cepisti veste Properti
    indue, nec vacuum flore relinque caput;
15 et pete, qua polles, ut sit tibi forma perennis,
    inque meum semper stent tibi regna caput.

PROPERTIUS III, x, 1–18 (with omissions)

l. 1 *quidnam:* 'why?' *Camenae:* the Muses'.
l. 2 *torum;* 'bed' *rubere:* 'to be red'.
l. 3 *natalis* (dies): 'birthday' *puella:* Cynthia.
l. 4 *faustus:* 'well-omened, lucky' *crepare:* 'to clap'.
l. 5 *aër, aëris:* 'air'.
l. 6 *siccum:* 'dry (land)'.
l. 8 *Niobae ipse lapis:* 'the very stone which is Niobe'; according to legend, when Niobe lost her children, she was turned to stone and wept for them forever.
l. 9 *felicibus edita pennis:* 'born under happy omens'; *pennae,* literally 'feathers', here means 'birds'; behaviour of birds was studied as a means of foretelling the future; we might say 'born under a happy star'.
l. 10 *iusta* (n.pl.) and *deos* are both objects of *precare;* 'make a just prayer to the gods, who demand it (*poscentes*)'.
l. 11 *lympha:* 'water'.
l. 12 *pollex, pollicis:* 'thumb' *fingere:* 'to shape', here 'to arrange'.
ll. 13–14 *qua . . . veste . . ., indue = vestem indue, qua . . .*
l. 15 *pollere:* 'to be powerful' *perennis:* 'lasting'.
l. 16 *in meum . . . caput:* 'over me'.

1. What surprised Propertius?
2. *sole rubente* (l. 2): what time of day does this suggest?
3. Why had the Muses come and what did they do?
4. It seems unlikely that Propertius in fact had a visit from the Muses. What actual experience do you suppose he describes in these terms?
5. Lines 5–8: summarize the meaning of these lines. What relevance do they have to the main theme of the poem?
6. Explain the meaning of *minas* (l. 6).
7. What does the reference to Niobe add to the meaning?
8. Lines 11–14: What does Propertius tell Cynthia to do (six things)?
9. What does he tell her to pray for (ll. 15–16)?
10. What do the words *polles* and *regna* (ll. 15, 16) suggest about the relations between Propertius and Cynthia?
11. What is the feeling of the poem as a whole?

14. Two heroes and an anti-hero

i. Caratacus

Caratacus, son of Cunobelinus, had led the resistance to Claudius' invasion of Britain (A.D. 43). After defeat in battle he had fled to Wales, where he carried on guerilla warfare. Eventually his forces were trapped and defeated; he escaped and took refuge with the Brigantes, the most powerful British tribe still undefeated by the Romans.

Ipse, cum fidem Cartimanduae reginae Brigantum petivisset, vinctus et victoribus traditus est, nono post anno quam bellum in Britannia coeptum est. Unde fama eius pervagata per Italiam quoque celebrabatur, ave-
5 bantque visere, quis ille tot per annos opes nostras sprevisset. Ne Romae quidem ignobile Carataci nomen erat; et Caesar dum suum decus extollit, addidit gloriam victo. Vocatus enim ut ad insigne spectaculum populus: stetere in armis praetoriae cohortes campo qui castra
10 praeiacet. Tunc incedentibus regiis clientulis, quae bellis externis quaesiverat traducta sunt, mox fratres et coniunx et filia, postremo ipse ostentatus. Ceterorum preces degeneres fuere ex metu: at non Caratacus aut vultu demisso aut verbis misericordiam requirens, ubi
15 tribunali adstitit, in hunc modum locutus est:

'Si res mihi prosperae fuissent, amicus potius in hanc urbem quam captus venissem, neque dedignatus esses me foedere in pacem accipere. Habui equos, viros, arma,
20 opes: quid mirum si haec invitus amisi? Nam si vos omnibus imperitare vultis, sequitur ut omnes servitutem accipiant?' Ad ea Caesar veniam ipsi et coniugi et fratribus tribuit.

TACITUS, *Annals* xii, 36–37

76

l. 1 *fides, fidei:* 'protection'.
l. 4 *pervagari:* 'to spread abroad'.
l. 5 *avere:* 'to be eager to'.
l. 6 *ignobilis:* 'unknown'.
l. 7 *extollere:* 'to raise, increase'.
l. 9 *praetoriae cohortes:* the emperor's bodyguard.
l. 10 *praeiacere:* 'to lie in front of' *regiis clientulis:* 'the vassal princes (of Caratacus)' *quae ... quaesiverat:* 'what he (the emperor) had won in foreign wars' i.e. booty *traducere:* 'to lead past, parade'.
l. 12 *ostentare:* 'to display' *degener:* 'degrading, shameful'.
l. 14 *demissus:* 'down cast' *misericordia:* 'mercy'.
l. 17 *dedignari:* 'to disdain'.
l. 19 *foedus, foederis:* 'treaty'.
l. 22 *venia:* 'pardon, mercy'.

1. Who was Cartimandua and how did she treat Caratacus?
2. In what year did these events take place?
3. Why did the people of Italy want to see Caratacus?
4. *et Caesar ... victo* (ll. 7–8): what was the emperor (Caesar) trying to do, and what did he in fact do?
5. Describe in the greatest possible detail the *spectaculum* to which the people were invited.
6. How did the other captives behave?
7. How did Caratacus behave?
8. What would have happened, according to Caratacus, if things had gone well for him?
9. Summarize the sense of his speech from *Habui* (l. 19) to *accipiant* (l. 22).
10. Which of the following best characterizes his speech: rash, impertinent, suppliant, defiant, prudent?
11. How did the emperor respond to this speech?
12. What feelings does the passage arouse in you towards (a) Caratacus (b) the emperor?

ii. The elder Pliny

In A.D. 79 Vesuvius erupted, burying the surrounding
district in ash and lava. Pliny writes to the historian Tacitus,
giving an account of what his uncle did during the eruption.

Erat Miseni classemque imperio praesens regebat.
Nonum kal. Septembres hora fere septima mater mea
indicat ei apparere nubem inusitata et magnitudine et
specie ... Magnum propiusque noscendum ut eruditis-
5 simo viro visum. Iubet liburnicam aptari; mihi si venire
una vellem facit copiam; respondi studere me malle, et
forte ipse quod scriberem dederat. Egrediebatur domo;
accipit codicillos Rectinae imminenti periculo exterritae
(nam villa eius subiacebat, nec ulla nisi navibus fuga):
10 ut se tanto discrimini eriperet orabat. Vertit ille consilium, et quod studioso animo incohaverat obit maximo.
Deducit quadriremes, ascendit ipse non Rectinae modo
sed multis aliis laturus auxilium. Properat illuc unde
alii fugiunt, rectumque cursum recta gubernacula in
15 periculum tenet. Iam navibus cinis incidebat, quo
propius accederent, calidior et densior; iam pumices
etiam nigrique et ambusti et fracti igne lapides; iam
vadum subitum ruinaque montis litora obstantia.
Cunctatus paulum an retro flecteret, mox gubernatori ut
20 ita faceret monenti 'Fortes' inquit 'fortuna iuvat:
Pomponianum pete.'

PLINY, *Ep.* VI, xvi, 4–11

(i) In what cases are the following words, and why:
Miseni (l. 1); *magnitudine* (l. 3); *domo* (l. 7); *Rectinae* (l. 8);
monenti (l. 20)?
(ii) Explain why *scriberem* (l. 7) and *flecteret* (l. 19) are in
the subjunctive mood.
(iii) *egrediebatur, accipit* (ll. 7–8): why does the tense
change?
(iv) *laturus* (l. 13): what part of the verb is this and what
does it here express?

l. 1   Misenum was a town on the opposite side of the bay of Naples to Vesuvius   *praesens:* 'present' i.e. 'in person'.

l. 2   *nonum kal. Septembres* = *ante diem nonum kalendas Septembres.*

l. 3   *apparere:* 'to appear'   *inusitatus:* 'unusual'.

l. 4   *species:* 'appearance'.

ll. 4–5   *Magnum . . . visum:* 'it seemed (to him) as a scholar an important phenomenon, worth closer investigation': he was a man of voracious curiosity, who had written, amongst other works, a massive Natural History.

l. 5   *liburnica:* 'a pinnace'.

l. 6   *copia:* 'opportunity'.

l. 8   *codicilli:* 'a letter'   Rectina was a friend of the family.

l. 10   *discrimen:* 'danger'.

l. 11   *quod studioso . . . maximo:* 'what he had begun from curiosity, he pursued from courage'.

l. 14   *rectus:* 'straight'   *gubernaculum:* 'helm'.

l. 15   *cinis:* 'ash'

l. 16   *pumex, pumicis:* 'volcanic stone'.

l. 17   *ambustus:* 'burnt'.

l. 18   *vadum:* 'a shallow, a shoal'   *ruina:* ablative case.

l. 18   *cunctari:* 'to delay, to hesitate'   *retro* (adv.): 'back'.

l. 20   Pomponianus was another friend in the danger area.

1. Where was Pliny's uncle, and what was his job at the time?
2. When precisely did the eruption take place?
3. How did it appear to those at Misenum?
4. What orders did Pliny's uncle give, and why?
5. Why did Pliny refuse to go with his uncle? What was he doing?
6. Why was Rectina in extreme danger? What did she ask Pliny's uncle to do?
7. Explain the meaning of *vertit ille consilium* (l. 10).
8. Describe in detail what happened as the ships approached the danger area.
9. *cunctatus* (l. 18): who hesitated, and why?
10. Explain the meaning of *ut ita faceret* (l. 19).
11. What impression of his uncle does Pliny wish to give? By which phrases is this impression most clearly conveyed?

iii. A poor fish

C. Canius, eques Romanus, cum se Syracusas contu-
lisset, dicebat se hortulos aliquos emere velle, quo
invitare amicos et ubi se oblectare sine interpellatoribus
posset. Quod cum percrebuisset, Pythius ei quidam, qui
5 argentariam faceret Syracusis, dixit venales quidem se
hortos non habere, sed licere uti Canio, si vellet, ut suis:
et simul ad cenam hominem in hortos invitavit. Cum
ille promisisset, tum Pythius piscatores ad se convocavit,
et ab iis petivit ut ante suos hortulos postridie piscaren-
10 tur, dixitque quid eos facere vellet. Ad cenam tempore
venit Canius. Cumbarum ante oculos multitudo; pro se
quisque, quod ceperat, adferebat; ante pedes Pythii
pisces abiciebantur. Tum Canius 'Quaeso,' inquit, 'quid
est hoc, Pythi? Tantumne piscium? tantumne cum-
15 barum?' Et ille 'Quid mirum?' inquit: 'hoc loco est
Syracusis quidquid est piscium.' Incensus Canius cupi-
ditate contendit a Pythio ut venderet. Recusavit ille
primo. Tandem tamen emit homo cupidus et locuples
tanti, quanti Pythius voluit. Invitat Canius postridie
20 familiares suos; venit ipse mature; cumbam nullam
videt. Quaerit a proximo vicino num feriae piscatorum
essent. 'Nullae, quod sciam' inquit: 'sed hic piscari nulli
solent. Itaque heri mirabar quid accidisset.' Stomachari
Canius. Sed quid faceret?

CICERO, de Officiis iii, 14

l. 2   *hortulus:* 'a little garden'.

l. 3   *se oblectare:* 'to enjoy himself'   *interpellator:* 'an interrupter'.

l. 4   *percrebescere:* 'to spread abroad'.

l. 5   *argentaria:* 'a bank'.

l. 5   *venalis:* 'for sale'.

l. 8   *piscator:* 'a fisherman'.

l. 11   *cumba:* 'a fishing boat'.

l. 16   *Syracusis quidquid est piscium:* 'all the fish there are at Syracuse'.

l. 17   *recusare:* 'to refuse'.

l. 18   *locuples:* 'rich'.

l. 21   *feriae, feriarum:* 'a holiday'.

l. 22   *quod sciam:* 'as far as I know'.

ll. 23–24   *stomachari Canius:* 'Canius was angry' (historic infinitive).

1. What did Canius say he wanted to do, and why?
2. What did Pythius offer to do for Canius?
3. To whom does *ille* (l. 8) refer? What did he promise?
4. What did Pythius ask the fishermen to do?
5. What did Canius find when he came to dinner?
6. How did Pythius explain what was happening?
7. Why was Canius now so anxious to buy the gardens?
8. How much did he pay for them?
9. What did he do next day?
10. What did he ask his neighbour?
11. What did the neighbour reply?
12. Describe the characters of Canius and Pythius as they are portrayed in this passage.

(i) In what cases are the following words? Show, by translation or explanation, why these caeses are used: *Syracusas* (l. 1); *quod* (l. 4); *Canio* (l. 6); *suis* (l. 6); *piscium* (l. 16); *tanti* (l. 19).

(ii) *Quid faceret* (l. 24): translate.

(iii) Examine the length of the sentences in this passage. Can you find any reason for the variation of sentence length?

15. Four glimpses of Britain

i. A letter to an officer serving under Julius Caesar in Britain

Ego te commendare non desisto, sed, quid proficiam ex te scire cupio. Spem maximam habeo in Balbo, ad quem de te diligentissime et saepissime scribo. Illud soleo admirari, non me toties accipere tuas litteras,
5 quoties a Quinto mihi fratre afferantur. In Britannia nihil esse audio neque auri neque argenti. Id si ita est, essedum aliquod suadeo capias et ad nos quam primum recurras. Sin autem sine Britannia tamen assequi, quod volumus, possumus, perfice ut sis in familiaribus
10 Caesaris. Multum te in eo frater adiuvabit meus, multum Balbus, sed, mihi crede, tuus pudor et labor plurimum. Imperatorem liberalissimum, aetatem opportunissimam, commendationem certe singularem habes, ut tibi unum timendum sit, ne ipse tibi defuisse
15 videare.

CICERO, *ad Fam.* vii, 7

l. 1 *te:* Cicero is writing to a young man called Trebatius
desistere: 'to stop'   *proficere:* 'to make progress'.
l. 2 Balbus was Caesar's confidential secretary in Rome.
l. 5 Cicero's brother Quintus was also serving in Britain.
l. 7 *essedum:* a British war chariot.
ll. 8–9 *Sin autem . . . possumus:* 'but if we can still achieve what
we want without (your staying in) Britain . . .
l. 11 *pudor:* 'modesty'.
l. 12 *liberalis:* 'generous'.
l. 13 *singularis:* 'unique'.
l. 15 *deesse:* 'to fail'.

1. What has Trebatius asked Cicero to do for him? Quote
   the Latin words which make this clear.
2. How does Cicero stress that he is doing all he can for
   Trebatius? Quote the relevant Latin; there are three
   relevant passages in the whole letter.
3. How does Cicero hope to hear whether he is succeeding?
4. What surprises Cicero (ll. 4–5)? What would be meant by
   saying that this sentence was ironical and mildly
   censorious?
5. What does Cicero hear about Britain? What does this and
   the following sentence suggest about Trebatius' motive
   for joining the campaign?
6. What does Cicero advise Trebatius to do? Does this seem
   to you a serious suggestion?
7. In the list of things which will help Trebatius (ll. 10–12),
   which is the most important? How does Cicero make this
   plain?
8. Translate *ut tibi . . . videare* (ll. 14–15). What is the tone of
   the last sentence?
9. What does this letter tell you about the character of
   Trebatius and about Cicero's attitude to him?

   (i) What is the function of *illud* (l. 3)?
   (ii) In what case are *auri* and *argenti* (l. 6)? Why?
   (iii) *essedum suadeo capias* (l. 7): what conjunction would
   you normally expect to find here? Why do you suppose
   essedum is in this position?

ii. Two inscriptions

(a) From the triumphal arch of Claudius in Rome

TIberio **CLAUDIO DRUSI** Filio **CAISARI
AUGUSTO GERMANICO PONTIFICI MAXIMO
TRIB**unicia **POTESTATE XI CO**nsuli **V IMPERAT-
ORI PATRI PATRIAE SENATUS POPULUSQUE**
5 **ROMANUS QUOD REGES BRITANNIAE XI
DEVICTOS SINE ULLA IACTURA IN DEDI-
TIONEM ACCEPERIT GENTESQUE BARBARAS
TRANS OCEANUM PRIMUS IN DICIONEM**
10 **POPULI ROMANI REDEGERIT**

The letters in small print are omitted from the actual inscription.

(b) A temple dedication from Britain

Cogidubnus (or Cogidumnus) was king of the Regni in west Sussex. He came over to the Romans and was rewarded by being allowed to keep his kingdom with the unique title *rex legatus Augusti*. Recently a large and magnificent villa has been excavated at Fishbourne, near Chichester, which was probably his palace.

**NEPTUNO ET MINERVAE TEMPLUM PRO
SALUTE DOMUS DIVINAE EX AUCTORITATE**
TIberii **CLAUD**ii **COGIDUBNI** Regis **LEGAT**i
AUGusti **IN BRIT**annia **COLLEGIUM FABROR**um
5 **ET QUI IN EO SUNT** De Suo Dederunt **DONANTE
AREAM CLEMENTE PUDENTINI** FILio.

From Chichester

l. 2 *domus divina:* i.e. the imperial family.
l. 2 *ex auctoritate:* 'on the authority of'.
l. 4 *collegium fabrorum:* 'the union of smiths'.
l. 5 *de suo:* 'from their own (money), at their own expense'
area: 'site'.

l. 2 *pontifex maximus:* 'high priest'   *tribunicia potestate XI:*
'holding the power of tribune for the eleventh time (i.e. A.D. 51–2).
  ll. 4–5 *senatus populusque Romanus:* supply 'dedicated this arch'.
  l. 6 *iactura:* 'loss'.
  l. 9 *dicio, dicionis:* dominion'.

1. Interpret Claudius' titles.
2. Why was the arch dedicated to him?
3. Compare the tone of this inscription with that of the
   following lines on Rome's imperial mission:
   > tu regere imperio populos, Romane, memento
   > (hae tibi erunt artes), paicisque imponere morem,
   > parcere subiectis et debellare superbos.
   >> VIRGIL, *Aeneid* vi, 851–3
   What differences of attitude do you see?

  l. 1 *memento:* 'remember' (imperative).
  l. 3 *debellare:* 'to overcome by war'.

1. Who dedicated the temple? and to what gods? Suggest
   why the donors should have chosen these particular gods.
2. What is meant by *pro salute domus divinae* (ll. 1–2)?
3. Explain the significance of the name and titles here given
   to Cogidubnus.
4. Tacitus, writing in A.D. 97 on the invasion of Britain, says:

   > Quaedam civitates Cogidumno regi donatae (is ad
   > nostram usque memoriam fidissimus mansit), vetere ac
   > iam pridem recepta populi Romani consuetudine, ut
   > haberet instrumenta servitutis et reges.

   (a) What information does Tacitus here give about
   Cogidumnus? How is this information attested by the
   inscription?
   (b) Explain Tacitus' comment *vetere . . . et reges*. Compare
   the tone of this comment with that of Claudius' triumphal
   inscription.

      l. 2 *iam pridem:* 'long ago'.
      l. 3 *consuetudo:* 'custom'.
      l. 4 *et reges:* 'even kings'.

iii. Tacitus on the Britons

Tacitus has been discussing the origin of the peoples of Britain.

In universum aestimanti Gallos vicinam insulam occupasse credibile est. Eorum sacra deprehendas ac superstitionum persuasionem; sermo haud multum diversus, in deposcendis periculis eadem audacia et, ubi
5 advenere, in detractandis eadem formido. Plus tamen ferociae Britanni praeferunt, ut quos nondum longa pax emollierit. Nam Gallos quoque in bellis floruisse accepimus; mox segnitia cum otio intravit, amissa virtute pariter ac libertate. Quod Britannorum olim victis
10 evenit: ceteri manent quales Galli fuerunt. In pedite robur; quaedam nationes et curru proeliantur. Olim regibus parebant, nunc per principes factionibus et studiis distrahuntur. Nec aliud adversus validissimas gentes pro nobis utilius quam quod in commune non
15 consulunt. Rarus duabus tribusve civitatibus ad propulsandum commune periculum conventus: ita singuli pugnant, universi vincuntur. Ipsi Britanni dilectum ac tributa et iniuncta imperii munia impigre obeunt, si iniuriae absint: has aegre tolerant, iam domiti ut
20 pareant, nondum ut serviant.

TACITUS, *Agricola* 11–13

l. 1   *in universum aestimanti:* literally 'to a person judging in general', i.e. 'to form a general judgement'.

l. 2   *occupasse = occupavisse   deprehendas:* 'you would find (among the Britons)'.

l. 3   *superstitionum persuasiones:* 'religious beliefs'.

l. 4   *deposcere:* 'to demand, challenge'   *eadem audacia:* supply *est.*

l. 5   *detractare:* 'to refuse, shrink from'.

l. 6   *praeferre:* 'to display'   *ut quos . . . emollierint:* 'because long peace has not yet made them soft'.

l. 8   *accipere:* 'to hear'   *segnitia:* 'slackness, lack of spirit'.

ll. 9–10   *Quod . . . evenit:* 'this has happened to (those) of the Britons conquered some time ago'.

l. 11   *robur:* 'strength'.

l. 11   *natio:* 'a tribe'.

ll. 12–13   *factiones et studia:* literally 'factions and party spirit'.

l. 14   *quam quod:* 'than the fact that . . .'

l. 15   *rarus (est) . . . conventus:* 'combination is rare' i.e. 'it is rare for . . . to combine'   *propulsare:* 'to repel'.

l. 17   *dilectus:* 'conscription'   *iniuncta imperii munia:* 'obligations imposed by the government'.

l. 19   *domare:* 'to tame, subdue'.

l. 20   *nondum:* 'not yet'.

1. Where does Tacitus believe the Britons came from? What three pieces of evidence does he give to support this view?
2. How, according to Tacitus, do the Britons compare with the Gauls as warriors? How does he account for what he says on this topic?
3. What was their political organization in the time of Tacitus?
4. What were the consequences of this political set-up?
5. Were they good subjects of the Roman empire?
6. Summarize the national characteristics which Tacitus ascribes to the Britons.

iv. A British lady in Rome

Claudia caeruleis cum sit Rufina Britannis
    edita, quam Latiae pectora gentis habet!
quale decus formae! Romanam credere matres
    Italides possunt, Atthides esse suam.
5   di bene, quod sancto peperit fecunda marito,
    quod sperat generos quodque puella nurus.
sic placeat superis ut coniuge gaudeat uno
    et semper natis gaudeat illa tribus.

MARTIAL xi, 53

The process of Romanization which could produce a
Rufina had been accelerated by Agricola, governor from 78
to 85.

Sequens hiems saluberrimis consiliis absumpta. Namque hortari privatim, adiuvare publice, ut templa fora
domos exstruerent. Iam vero principum filios liberalibus
artibus erudire, et ingenia Britannorum studiis Gallorum
5 anteferre, ut, qui modo linguam Romanam abnuebant,
eloquentiam concupiscerent. Inde etiam habitus nostri
honor et frequens toga.

TACITUS, Agricola 21

l. 1 *caeruleus:* 'blue'   *cum:* 'although'.

l. 2 *edita:* 'born from' i.e. 'daughter of'   *quam:* 'How...!'
(exclamatory).

ll. 3–4 *Romanam...possunt=matres Italides credere possunt eam
Romanam esse.*

l. 4 *Atthides:* 'Athenian (mothers)'.

l. 5 *di bene:* 'heaven be praised!'   *peperit:* 'she has borne
children'   *fecundus:* 'fertile'.

l. 6 *gener:* 'a son-in-law'   *nurus- us:* 'a daughter-in-law'.

1. What strikes you as significant about Claudia Rufina's
   name?
2. What surprises Martial about her? Why is he so surprised?
3. Explain the meaning of *Romanam credere... esse suam*
   (ll. 3–4).
4. Summarize the qualities which Martial admires in
   Rufina.
5. How many children had she? Were they all boys or all
   girls or some of each? How do you know?
6. What is Martial's final prayer on her behalf? Is there an
   implied criticism?

l. 1 *sequens hiems:* i.e. winter 79   *saluber:* 'healthy, sound'.

l. 2 *hortari... adiuvare:* the infinitives in this passage are historic: 'he (Agricola) encouraged...'

l. 3 *iam vero:* 'moreover'.

l. 4 *erudire:* 'to train'   *ingenia,* n.pl.: 'natural talents'.

l. 5 *anteferre:* 'to prefer'   *ut, qui modo...:* 'so that (those) who
lately...'

ll. 5–6 *abnuere:* 'to refuse, to reject'   *habitus -us:* 'dress'.

l. 7 *frequens:* 'common'.

1. How did Agricola foster the Romanization of the
   Britons?
2. What aspects of Roman life did he encourage?
3. What were the results of this policy?

16. A millionaire's dinner party

i. Some guests arrive

His repleti voluptatibus cum conaremur in triclinium intrare, exclamavit unus ex pueris, qui super hoc officium erat positus: 'dextro pede.' Sine dubio paulisper trepidavimus, ne contra praeceptum aliquis nostrum
5 limen transiret. Ceterum ut pariter movimus dextros gressus, servus nobis despoliatus procubuit ad pedes ac rogare coepit, ut se poenae eriperemus: nec magnum esse peccatum suum, propter quod periclitaretur; subducta enim sibi vestimenta dispensatoris in balneo, quae
10 vix fuissent decem sestertiorum. Rettulimus ergo dextros pedes dispensatoremque in oecario aureos numerantem deprecati sumus, ut servum remitteret poenam. Superbus ille sustulit vultum et 'Non tam iactura me movet' inquit 'quam neglegentia nequissimi servi. Vestimenta
15 mea cubitoria perdidit, quae mihi natali meo cliens quidam donaverat, Tyria sine dubio, sed iam semel lota. Quid ergo est? Dono vobis eum.'

Obligati tam grandi beneficio cum intrassemus triclinium, occurrit nobis ille idem servus, pro quo
20 rogaveramus, et stupentibus nobis spississima basia impegit, gratias agens humanitati nostrae. 'Statim scietis' ait 'cui dederitis beneficium. Vinum dominicum ministratoris gratia est.'

PETRONIUS, *Satyricon* 30–31

(i) In what cases are the following words and why: *nostrum* (l. 4): *nobis* (l. 6); *sibi* (l. 9); *sestertiorum* (l. 10); *natali meo* (l. 15).

(ii) *nec magnum esse peccatum suum* (ll. 7–8): why is the infinitive used here?

(iii) Distinguish the uess of *ut*: *ut . . . movimus* (l. 5), *ut . . . eriperemus* (l. 7).

l. 1 *his voluptatibus:* before entering the dining room, the guests have been inspecting the beauties of the hall.

l. 3 *paulisper:* 'for a little'   *praeceptum:* 'instruction'.

l. 5 *limen:* 'threshold'   *ceterum:* 'but'.

l. 6 *despoliatus:* 'stripped'.

l. 8 *peccatum:* 'sin, crime'   *periclitari:* 'to be in danger'.

ll. 8–9 *subducere:* 'to remove, steal'   *dispensator:* 'accountant'.

l. 11 *oecarium:* 'office'   *deprecari:* 'to intercede, to plead'.

l. 13 *iactura:* 'loss'.

l. 14 *nequissiumus:* 'utterly worthless'   *vestimenta cubitoria:* 'dinner clothes'.

l. 15 *natalis (dies)*: 'birthday'   *cliens:* 'a dependent'; a *cliens* was a poor man who was under the protection of a wealthy patron *Tyria:* i.e. made in Tyre, or of Tyrian purple, a very expensive dye *lotus:* 'washed'.

l. 20 *stupere:* 'to be dumbfounded'   *spississima basia impegit:* 'planted a shower of kisses'   *dominicus:* 'of the master'.

1. What happened when the guests tried to enter the dining room?
2. How did they react to this, and why?
3. Explain the meaning of *ut pariter movimus dextros gressus* (ll. 5–6). What picture do these words give? Where is the phrase echoed later in the passage?
4. Why do you suppose the slave (l. 6) was *despoliatus*? What did he ask them to do?
5. What was the slave's *peccatum*?
6. Translate *quae vix fuissent decem sestertiorum* (l. 10). Does this suggest that the clothes were cheap or expensive?
7. What was the *dispensator* doing when they found him?
8. What did they ask him to do?
9. How does the *dispensator* describe his clothes?
10. How did the slave show his gratitude, and how did he propose to repay them?
11. The accountant is described as *superbus*; how does this quality show itself?
12. Tell the story of the loss of the clothes, in English, (a) as the slave (b) as the accountant would have told it.

The host is Trimalchio (see 4, i).

ii. A guest's story

The speaker is called Niceros.

'Cum adhuc servirem, habitabamus in vico angusto. Ibi amare coepi uxorem Terentii cauponis: noveratis Melissam, pulcherrimum bacciballum. Huius contubernalis ad villam supremum diem obiit. Itaque per scutum
5 per ocream egi aginavi, quomodo ad illam pervenirem: scitis autem in angustiis amici apparent. Forte dominus Capuam exierat ad scruta scita expedienda. Nactus ego occasionem, persuadeo hospitem nostrum ut mecum ad quintum milarium veniat. Erat autem miles, fortis quam
10 Orcus. Apoculamus nos circa gallicinia, luna lucebat tamquam meridie. Venimus inter monimenta: homo meus coepit ad stelas facere; sedeo ego cantabundus et stelas numero. Deinde ut respexi ad comitem, ille exuit se et omnia vestimenta secundum viam posuit. Mihi
15 anima in naso erat, stabam tamquam mortuus. At ille subito lupus factus est. Nolite me iocari putare; postquam lupus factus est, ululare coepit et in silvas fugit. Ego primum nesciebam ubi essem, deinde accessi, ut vestimenta eius tollerem; illa autem lapidea facta sunt.
20 Quis mori timore nisi ego? Gladium tamen strinxi et in tota via umbras cecidi, donec ad villam amicae meae pervenirem. Ut larva intravi, oculi mortui, vix unquam refectus sum. Melissa mea mirari coepit, quod tam sero ambularem, et "Si ante" inquit "venisses, saltem nos
25 adiuvisses; lupus enim villam intravit et omnia pecora tamquam lanius sanguinem illis misit. Nec tamen derisit, etiam si fugit; servus enim noster lancea collum eius traiecit." Haec ut audivi, operire oculos amplius non potui, sed luce clara domum fugi, et postquam veni in
30 illum locum, in quo lapidea vestimenta erant facta, nihil inveni nisi sanguinem. Ut vero domum veni, iacebat miles meus in lecto et collum eius medicus curabat.

l. 1   *vicus:* 'street'.

l. 2   *caupo, cauponis:* 'inn keeper'.

l. 3   *bacciballum:* 'a peach'   *contubernalis:* 'husband'   *ad villam:* 'on the farm'.

ll. 4–5   *per scutum . . . aginavi:* 'I struggled and strove by hook and by crook . . .'

l. 6   *angustiae:* 'difficulties'.

l. 7   *ad scruta scita expedienda:* 'to deal with some odds and ends'.

l.9   *milarium:* 'mile-stone'   *Orcus:* 'hell'   *apoculamus circa gallicinia:* 'we toddle off around cock-crow'.

l. 11   *monimentum:* 'a tomb'; Roman tombs were usually along the road just outside the town   *stela:* 'a grave stone'.

l. 12   *facere ad:* 'to make for'   *cantabundus:* 'singing'.

l. 14   *secundum* (prep. with acc.): 'beside'   *anima:* 'spirit, heart' *nasus:* 'nose'.

l. 16   *iocari:* 'to joke'   *ululare:* 'to howl'.

l. 19   *lapideus -a-um:* 'stone'.

l. 22   *ut larva:* 'like a ghost'.

l. 26   *lanius:* 'a butcher'.

ll. 26–27   *nec tamen derisit:* 'but he didn't get the last laugh'.

l. 27   *collum:* 'neck'.

l. 28   *operire:* 'to close'.

1. Why was Niceros so anxious to go to Melissa on this occasion?
2. What gave him the opportunity of going?
3. Who went with him? What sort of person was his companion?
4. When they reached the graveyard, what did Niceros' companion do first and what did Niceros do?
5. When Niceros looked up, what was his companion doing?
6. Express in natural English: *Mihi anima . . . mortuus* (ll. 14–15).
7. What happened to the soldier's clothes?
8. How did Niceros then feel, and how did he behave on the rest of the journey?
9. Why was Melissa surprised when she first saw him?
10. What news had she for him?
11. What effect did the news have on Niceros? Why?
12. What did he find when he reached home?

Intellexi illum versipellem esse, nec postea cum illo panem gustare potui, non si me occidisses.'

PETRONIUS, Satyricon 61–62

iii. An abortive attempt to leave

In the middle of the dinner their host has just suggested that they should all take a bath.

Ego respiciens ad Ascylton 'Quid cogitas?' inquam, 'ego enim si videro balneum, statim exspirabo.' 'Assentemur,' ait ille, 'et dum illi balneum petunt, nos in turba exeamus.' Cum haec placuissent, ducente per
5 porticum Gitone ad ianuam venimus, ubi canis catenarius tanto nos tumultu excepit, ut Ascyltos etiam in piscinam ceciderit. Nec non ego quoque ebrius, dum natanti opem fero, in eundem gurgitem tractus sum. Servavit nos tamen atriensis, qui interventu suo et canem
10 placavit et nos trementes extraxit in siccum. Et Giton quidem iam dudum se ratione acutissima redemerat a cane; quidquid enim a nobis acceperat de cena, latranti sparserat. At ille, avocatus cibo, furorem suppresserat. Ceterum cum algentes petissemus ab atriense,
15 ut nos extra ianuam emitteret, 'Erras' inquit, 'si putas te exire hac posse qua venisti. Nemo unquam convivarum per eandem ianuam emissus est; alia intrant, alia exeunt.' Quid faciamus homines miserrimi et novi generis labyrintho inclusi, quibus lavari iam coeperat
20 votum esse? Ultro ergo rogavimus ut nos ad balneum duceret.

PETRONIUS, Satyricon 72

13. What is a *versipelles* (l. 34)?
14. On hearing this story, the host said 'my hair stood on end.' What effect does the story have on you?
15. The story is told in 'vulgar' Latin i.e. the ordinary language of the man in the street. What difference do you see from the literary language, in which most surviving Latin works are written?

l. 3   *assentari:* 'to agree'.
l. 5   *porticus -us:* 'a colonnade'   *ianua:* 'a door'.
l. 5   *catenarius:* 'chained'.
l. 7   *piscina:* 'an ornamental pool'   *ebrius:* 'drunk'.
l. 8   *gurges, gurgitis:* 'whirl pool, gulf'.
l. 9   *atriensis:* 'the doorkeeper'.
l. 10   *siccum:* 'dry land'.
l. 11   *iam dudum:* 'some time ago'.
l. 13   *latrare:* 'to bark'.
l. 14   *ceterum:* 'but'   *algere:* 'to be cold'.
l. 16   *conviva:* 'a guest'.
l. 20   *ultro:* 'of one's own accord'.

1. How did Encolpius (*ego*) feel about taking a bath?
2. What did Ascyltos suggest?
3. What happened to Ascyltos when they reached the door?
4. What happened to Encolpius, and why?
5. How were they rescued?
6. How had Giton saved himself?
7. What did they ask the door-keeper?
8. What did the door-keeper reply?
9. *novi generis labyrintho inclusi* (ll. 18–19): translate. What was the original labyrinth? Why is the word used here?
10. What did they finally ask the door-keeper to do, and why?
11. Give a brief summary of the events described in this passage. Show how Petronius has embroidered 'the facts' and suggest why he does so.

(i) Distinguish the meanings of the subjunctive: *exeamus* (l. 4), *faciamus* (l. 18).
(ii) Distinguish the uses of *ut: ut . . . ceciderit* (ll. 6–7); *ut . . . emitteret* (l. 15).
(iii) In what cases are the following words, and why: *ducente* (l. 4); *natanti* (l. 8); *alia* (l. 17); *quibus* (l. 19)?

17. Politics

i. A debate in the senate

The consul, Cicero, has obtained clear evidence of a revolutionary conspiracy and has arrested some of the ring-leaders.

Consul convocato senatu refert quid de eis fieri placeat, qui in custodiam traditi erant. Tum D. Iunius Silanus primus sententiam rogatus, quod eo tempore consul designatus erat, de eis, qui in custodia tenebantur,
5 supplicium sumendum esse decrevit. Sed Caesar, ubi ad eum ventum est, rogatus a consule sententiam, huiusce modi verba locutus est:

'Omnes homines, patres conscripti, qui de rebus dubiis consultant, ab odio, amicitia, ira atque misericordia
10 vacuos esse decet ... Sed ita censeo, publicandas esse eorum pecunias, ipsos in vinculis habendos esse per municipia.'

Postquam Caesar dicendi finem fecit, ceteri verbo alius alii varie adsentiebantur. At M. Porcius Cato
15 rogatus sententiam huiusce modi orationem habuit:

'Longe mihi alia mens est, patres conscripti, cum res atque pericula nostra considero ... Quare ita censeo: cum nefario consilio sceleratorum civium res publica in maxima pericula venerit eique confessi sint se caedem,
20 incendia aliaque crudelia facinora in cives patriamque paravisse, de confessis more maiorum supplicium sumendum esse.'

Postquam Cato adsedit, consulares omnes itemque senatus magna pars sententiam eius laudant; senatus
25 decretum fit, sicuti ille censuerat.

SALLUST, *Catiline*, 50–53 passim

l. 1   *referre:* 'to put the question'.
l. 4   *consul designatus:* 'consul designate', i.e. he had been elected consul and would come into office the following January.
l. 5   *supplicium:* 'punishment'; here 'the death penalty'.
l. 10   *publicare:* 'to confiscate'.
l. 11   *municipium:* an Italian town.
l. 14   *adsentiri* + dative: 'to agree with'.
l. 18   *nefarius:* 'criminal, wicked'.
l. 23   *item:* 'in the same way, likewise'.

1. What was the consul's function in this debate?
2. What was the question put to the senate for debate?
3. Who spoke first? Why was he called first? What did he propose?
4. Who are the *patres conscripti* (l. 8)? How did they get this name?
5. What is the point of the opening sentence of Caesar's speech?
6. What did Caesar propose?
7. How did the senate react to Caesar's proposal?
8. What was Cato's proposal? On what grounds did he take this view?
9. How did the senate react to Cato's proposal and what was their final decision?
10. Deduce from this passage all that you can about the procedure for a debate in the senate. How is the procedure like and unlike that in the House of Commons?

(i) In what cases are the following words and why: *sententiam* (l. 3); *omnes homines* (l. 8); *alii* (l. 14); *nefario consilio* (l. 18)?

(ii) Explain the meaning and grammar of *ventum est* (l. 6).

(iii) Distinguish the meanings of *cum: cum considero* (ll. 16–17); *cum . . . venerit* (ll. 18–19).

ii. A rowdy meeting

Cicero writes to his brother Quintus, describing an assembly of the people before whom Clodius was prosecuting Milo; Pompey was supporting Milo.

Ante diem VII Id. Febr. Milo adfuit. Dixit Pompeius, sive voluit; nam, ut surrexit, operae Clodianae clamorem sustulerunt, idque ei perpetua oratione contigit. Qui ut peroravit (nam in eo sane fortis fuit; non est
5 deterritus; dixit omnia atque interdum etiam silentio, cum auctoritate pervicerat)—sed ut peroravit, surrexit Clodius. Ei tantus clamor a nostris (placuerat enim referre gratiam) ut neque mente neque lingua neque ore consisteret. Ea res acta est, cum hora sexta Pompeius
10 perorasset, usque ad horam octavam, cum omnia maledicta versusque obscenissimi in Clodium dicerentur. Ille furens et exsanguis interrogabat suos in clamore ipso quis esset qui plebem fame necaret; respondebant operae 'Pompeius'. Hora fere nona quasi signo dato
15 Clodiani nostros consputare coeperunt; exarsit dolor. Urgere illi ut loco nos moverent; factus est a nostris impetus; fuga operarum; eiectus de rostris Clodius, ac nos quoque tum fugimus, ne quid in turba. Senatus vocatus in curiam: Pompeius domum.

CICERO, *ad Quintum fratrem*, II, iii

l. 1 *adfuit:* literally 'was present', i.e. 'appeared in court'.
l. 2 *voluit:* supply *dicere.*   *operae Clodianae:* 'Clodius' gangs'.
l. 3 *perpetua oratione:* 'throughout his whole speech'.
l. 4 *perorare:* 'to end a speech'   *sane:* 'certainly'.
l. 5 *interdum:* 'from time to time'.
l. 7 *Ei tantus clamor:* 'Such a din (was made) at him . . .'
l. 8 *referre gratiam:* 'to repay the compliment'.
ll. 8–9 *ut neque mente . . . consisteret:* 'that he could not control his mind'.
l. 10 *maledictum:* 'abuse'.
l. 12 *exsanguis:* 'bloodless, pale'.
l. 13 *quis esset . . . necaret:* Pompey was at this time in charge of the corn supply.
l. 15 *consputare:* 'to spit at'   *exarsit dolor:* 'tempers flared up'.
l. 16 *urgere:* 'to shove'.
l. 17 *rostra* (n. pl.): the speaker's platform.

1. How did the *operae Clodianae* (l. 2) behave when Pompey spoke?
2. How did Pompey manage under these conditions?
3. How did *nostri* behave when Clodius got up? Why did they do this?
4. How long did this behaviour continue?
5. How did Clodius react to this reception?
6. What did Clodius ask the meeting? What was the point of his question?
7. What did Clodius' supporters do at the ninth hour? Explain what is meant by *quasi signo dato* (l. 14).
8. Describe the final stages of the meeting.
9. What strikes you about the way the last part is written? Why does Cicero write in this way?
10. Would you consider such a meeting a healthy symptom of a democratic system? On what occasions might you find such a meeting to-day?

(i) Explain the reference of the following pronouns: *id* (l. 3); *in eo* (l. 4); *ei* (l. 7).

(ii) *urgere* (l. 16): what use of the infinitive is this? How do you know?

(iii) *ne quid in turba* (l. 18): supply a suitable verb in the correct form in Latin.

iii. Election procedure

This extract is from the fifty-fifth paragraph of a long inscription containing the charter of the Spanish town of Malaca; by this charter the town was given the status of a *municipium*, i.e. a town of Roman citizens.

LV   De suffragio ferendo

Qui comitia ex hac lege habebit, is municipes curiatim ad suffragium ferendum vocato, ita ut uno vocatu omnes curias in suffragium vocet, eaeque singulae in singulis consaeptis suffragium per tabellam ferant. Itemque
5 curato, ut ad sistam cuiusque curiae ex municipibus eius municipi terni sint, qui eius curiae non sint, qui suffragia custodiant diribeant, et ut, antequam id faciant, quisque eorum iuret, se rationem suffragiorum fide bona habiturum relaturumque. Neve prohibeto quominus et ei qui
10 honorem petent singulos custodes ad singulas cistas ponant . . . Qua in curia totidem suffragia duo pluresve habuerint, maritum caelibi, habentem liberos non habenti, plures liberos habentem pauciores habenti praeferto.

Municipal charter from Malaca in
Spain, dated to A.D. 81

iv. An election poster

M. Epidium Sabinum duovirum iure dicundo oro vos faciatis, dignus est, defensorem coloniae, ex sententia Suedi Clementis sancti iudicis, consensu ordinis, ob merita eius et probitatem, dignum rei publicae. Faciatis.

From Pompeii, Dessau 6438d

l. 2   *suffragium:* 'vote'.

l.1   *comitia* (n.pl.): 'elections'   *Qui ... habebit, is ...*: 'the person who shall supervise elections in accordance with this law ...'

l. 2   *vocato:* third person imperative; 'is to call'; so also, *curato, ut* (l. 5): 'he is to see that ...'; and *Neve prohibeto:* 'he should not prevent ...' (l. 11).

l. 3   *curiae;* l. 1   *curiatim: curiae* are voting units; in Roman elections votes were cast by groups, not by individuals; the electors assemble *curiatim,* 'by groups' to decide how the group vote should be cast.

ll. 3–4   *eaeque singulae in singulis consaeptis:* 'and they (the *curiae*) separately in separate votings booth ...'   *tabella:* 'voting tablet'.

l. 5   *sista:* 'ballot box'   *terni:* 'three each' i.e. three citizens at each ballot box.

l. 7   *diribere:* 'to sort, count'.

l. 9   *relaturumque: referre:* 'to report'.

l. 11   *honos:* 'office'.

l. 13   *totidem* (indecl. adj.): 'the same number of ...'

l. 14   *caelebs, caelebis:* 'batchelor'.

l. 15   *praeferto:* imperative 'he shall prefer', this verb governs *maritum caelibi* as well as the following phrases.

1. Explain the procedure described in the first sentence.
2. What are the duties of the three citizens stationed at the ballot box of each *curia*? What do they have to swear?
3. What are the candidates permitted to do (ll. 10–11)? Why should they wish to do this?
4. What is to happen if two or more candidates have the same number of votes?
5. Does the procedure laid down in this passage seem to you fair and sensible? In what respects is it like and unlike procedure in a modern municipal or parliamentary election?

Most *municipia* elected four magistrates each year—two for judicial administration (*duoviri iure dicundo*), two for general administration (*aediles*)

oro vos faciatis: 'I ask you to elect'
ordo: 'the town council'.

1. For what office is Epidius standing?
2. What support does he claim?
3. What qualities are said to recommend him?

18. City life

i. A statesman's view

Cicero is coming to the end of his year of office as governor of Cilicia; he writes to M. Caelius Rufus, who is in Rome.

Sollicitus eram de rebus urbanis; ita tumultuosae contiones, ita molestae Quinquatrus adferebantur; sed tamen nihil me magis sollicitabat quam in iis molestiis non me, si quae ridenda essent, ridere tecum; sunt enim
5 multa, sed ea non audeo scribere. Illud moleste fero, nihil me adhuc his de rebus habere tuarum litterarum. Quare, etsi, cum tu haec leges, ego iam annuum munus confecero, tamen obviae mihi velim sint tuae litterae, quae me erudiant de omni re publica, ne hospes
10 plane veniam. Hoc melius quam tu facere nemo potest.

Urbem, urbem, mi Rufe, cole et in ista luce vive; omnis peregrinatio, quod ego ab adulescentia iudicavi, obscura et sordida est iis, quorum industria Romae potest illustris esse. Cum una mehercule ambulatiuncula atque
15 uno sermone nostro omnes fructus provinciae non confero. Sed, ut spero, propediem te videbo. Tu mihi obviam mitte epistulas te dignas.

CICERO, *ad Fam.*, ii, 12

(i) What is the function of *illud* (l. 5) ?

(ii) Translate *obviae . . . erudiant* (ll. 8–9): explain the uses of the subjunctives *velim, sint, erudiant.*

(iii) In what cases are the following words, and why: *nihil* (l. 3); *nihil* (l. 6); *litterarum* (l. 6); *te* (l. 17) ?

ll. 1–2   At this time (50 B.C.), the split between Caesar and the senate was widening and politics were becoming increasingly violent and bitter. Civil war broke out soon after Cicero had returned to Italy.

l. 1   *eram:* 'I was anxious (when I wrote this letter)'; we should say 'I am anxious'.

l. 2   *contio:* 'a public meeting'   *Quinquatrus:* a five day public holiday   *adferre:* 'to report'.

ll. 6–7   *nihil . . . tuarum litterarum:* 'no letter from you'.

ll. 7–8   *annuum munus:* 'my year's office'   *obvius -a-um:* 'meeting, to meet'; *obviam* is used as the adverb.

l. 9   *erudire:* 'to instruct, inform'.

ll. 9–10   *hospes plane:* literally 'simply a guest' i.e. 'an absolute stranger'.

l. 12   *peregrinatio:* 'foreign travel, foreign service'   *quod:* 'as'.

l. 14   *mehercule:* literally 'by Hercules', used to emphasize what is being said   *ambulatiuncula:* 'a little walk'.

l. 15   *sermone nostro:* 'talk together'.

ll. 15–16   *conferre:* 'to compare'   *propediem:* 'soon'.

1. Explain what is meant by *res urbanae* (l. 1). Why was Cicero worried?
2. What vexed him most?
3. Explain what is meant by *sunt enim . . . scribere* (ll. 4–5). Suggest why he says *ea non audeo scribere*.
4. What does he want Caelius to do for him, and what reasons does he give?
5. What does he advise Rufus (Caelius) to do? Why does he repeat *urbem*?
6. What does *in ista luce* (l. 11) mean? By which words is the metaphor picked up in the following sentence?
7. *Cum una . . . confero* (ll. 14–16): paraphrase this sentence in English.
8. *epistulas te dignas* (l. 17): where has the idea contained in *te dignas* occurred earlier in the letter?
9. Summarize Cicero's reasons for wishing to be in Rome.
10. What do you learn from the letter about Cicero's character? Do you find the views here expressed irreconcilable with those expressed in 2, i (Arpinum)?

ii. A rich man's view

C. Plinius Minicio Fundano suo S.

Mirum est quam singulis diebus in urbe ratio aut
constet aut constare videatur, pluribus iunctisque non
constet. Nam si quem interroges 'Hodie quid egisti?',
5 respondeat: 'officio togae virilis interfui, sponsalia aut
nuptias frequentavi, ille me ad signandum testamentum,
ille in advocationem, ille in consilium rogavit.' Haec quo
die feceris, necessaria, eadem, si cotidie fecisse te reputes,
iania videntur, multo magis cum secesseris. Tunc enim
10 subit recordatio: 'Quot dies quam frigidis rebus absumpsi!' Quod evenit mihi, postquam in Laurentino
meo aut lego aliquid aut scribo. Nihil audio quod
audisse, nihil dico quod dixisse paeniteat; nemo apud
me quemquam sinistris sermonibus carpit, neminem
15 ipse reprehendo, nisi tamen me, cum parum commode
scribo; nulla spe nullo timore sollicitor, nullis rumoribus
inquietor: mecum tantum et cum libellis loquor ...
Proinde tu quoque strepitum istum inanemque discur-
sum et ineptos labores, ut primum fuerit occasio,
20 relinque teque studiis vel otio trade. Satius est enim
otiosum esse quam nihil agere. Vale.

PLINY, *Ep.*, i, 9

(i) *si quem interroges, . . . respondeat* (ll. 4–5): translate and
explain the use of the subjunctive.
(ii) Distinguish the following pronouns: *quem* (l. 4); *aliquid*
(l. 12); *quemquam* (l. 14).
(iii) *fuerit* (l. 19): what part of the verb is this? Why is this
tense used?

ll. 1–2 *Mirum est . . . constet:* 'It is surprising how in the city day by day the accounts (of life) are balanced . . .' i.e. 'life makes sense' (a metaphor from book-keeping).

ll. 5–7 In this sentence Pliny reviews various duties (*officia*) mostly of social life   *togae virilis:* when a Roman boy came of age, between the ages of fourteen and sixteen, he laid down his purple-edged *toga* (*toga praetexta*) and assumed the plain white man's *toga*. *sponsalia:* betrothal or engagement ceremony   *frequentare:* 'to celebrate, attend'   *ad signandum testamentum:* 'to witness the signing of a will' (seven witnesses were required by law)   *in advocationem:* 'to give legal assistance' (as an advocate in court).

l. 7 *in consilium:* 'to join the judicial bench' i.e. to help a magistrate in a civil case as assessor.

l. 9 *inanis:* 'empty, pointless'   *multo magis cum secesseris:* 'all the more so when you have retired (to the country)'.

l. 10 *frigidus:* 'cold, dull'.

l. 11 Laurentinum: Pliny's country house at Laurentium, about 18 miles from Rome.

l. 13 *paeniteat:* supply *me:* 'I would regret'   *sinister:* 'unkind'.

l. 14 *carpere:* 'to carp at'.

l. 15 *parum commode:* literally 'too little suitably' i.e. 'inadequately, badly'.

l. 17 *inquietare:* 'to disquiet'.

l. 18 *proinde:* 'and so' *strepitus:* 'noise, din'   *discursus:*' dashing about'.

l. 19 *ineptus:* 'silly'.

l. 20 *satius est:* 'it is better'.

1. *Mirum est . . . :* explain what surprises Pliny.
2. *Nam si . . . absumpsi!* (ll. 4–11). How does Pliny account for this feeling of dissatisfaction?
3. How does Pliny spend his time in his country house?
4. What are the characteristics of life in his country house as opposed to life in the city?
5. What does he advise Fundanus to do?
6. What is the point of the last sentence? Does the letter suggest that Pliny was an idler?
7. In lines 18–19, Pliny characterizes city life by three phrases; consider how far these characteristics apply to city life to-day.

iii. A poor man's view

The speaker has had enough of life in Rome, living in the top storey of a block of flats. He intends to move to the country.

Quis timet, aut timuit, gelida Praeneste ruinam
aut positis nemorosa inter iuga Volsiniis aut
simplicibus Gabiis aut proni Tiburis arce?
nos urbem colimus tenui tibicine fultam
5 magna parte sui; nam sic labentibus obstat
vilicus, et veteris rimae cum texit hiatum,
securos pendente iubet dormire ruina.
vivendum illic est ubi nulla incendia, nulli
nocte metus. iam poscit aquam, iam frivola transfert
10 Ucalegon, tabulata tibi iam tertia fumant:
tu nescis; nam si gradibus trepidatur ab imis,
ultimus ardebit, quem tegula sola tuetur
a pluvia, molles ubi reddunt ova columbae . . .
si potes avelli circensibus, optima Sorae
15 aut Fabrateriae domus aut Frusinone paratur,
quanti nunc tenebras unum conducis in annum.

JUVENAL, Satires iii, 190–202, 223–5

l. 1   *gelida Praeneste*: 'in cool Praeneste'; Praeneste, Volsinii, Gabii and Tibur are all country towns fairly near Rome   *ruina:* 'collapse' (of buildings).

l. 2   *nemorosa iuga:* 'wooded hills'.

l. 3   *pronus:* 'sloping'.

l. 4   *tibicen, tibicinis:* 'a prop'   *fulcire:* 'to support'.

l. 5   *labentibus:* 'tottering (buildings)'.

l. 6   *vilicus:* 'agent'   *veteris rimae hiatus:* literally 'the gaping of the old crack'.

l. 8   *illic:* i.e. in the country.

l. 9   *frivola* (n.pl.): 'bits and pieces'.

l. 10   *Ucalegon:* i.e. your next door neighbour   *tabulata* (n.pl.): 'storey'.

l. 11   *gradibus trepidatur ab imis:* 'there is panic at the bottom of the stairs'.

l. 12   *tegula:* 'roof tile'.

l. 13   *pluvia:* 'rain'   *columba:* 'dove'.

l. 14   *avellere:* 'to tear away'.

l. 15   *paratur:* literally 'is obtained' i.e. 'can be bought'.

l. 16   *conducere:* 'to hire, rent'.

1. What characteristic do three of the towns mentioned in lines 1–3 have in common?
2. What is the matter with most of the houses in Rome, according to Juvenal? Quote the four phrases which ram this point home, and explain each of them.
3. What does the agent tell the tenants to do?
4. What, according to Juvenal, is the second great danger of living in Rome?
5. What is Ucalegon doing?
6. Who will suffer last, and why?
7. *molles . . . colombae* (l. 13): what grounds might there be for saying this clause was inappropriate here? What answer could you make to this view?
8. How much would a house cost at Sora? Explain what is meant by *tenebras* (l. 16).
9. Summarize the advantages of living in the country, according to Juvenal, and the disadvantages of living in Rome. Is there anything he is likely to miss in the country?

19. Country life

i. The farmer

Agricola incurvo terram dimovit aratro:
hic anni labor, hinc patriam parvosque nepotes
sustinet, hinc armenta boum meritosque iuvencos.
nec requies, quin aut pomis exuberet annus
5   aut fetu pecorum aut Cerealis mergite culmi,
proventuque oneret sulcos atque horrea vincat.
venit hiems: teritur Sicyonia baca trapetis,
glande sues laeti redeunt, dant arbuta silvae;
et varios ponit fetus autumnus, et alte
10 mitis in apricis coquitur vindemia saxis.
interea dulces pendent circum oscula nati,
casta pudicitiam servat domus, ubera vaccae
lactea demittunt, pinguesque in gramine laeto
inter se adversis luctantur cornibus haedi.
15 ipse dies agitat festos fususque per herbam,
ignis ubi in medio et socii cratera coronant,
te libans, Lenaee, vocat, pecorisque magistris
velocis iaculi certamina ponit in ulmo,
corporaque agresti nudant praedura palaestra.
20 aureus hanc vitam in terris Saturnus agebat;
necdum etiam audierant inflari classica, necdum
impositos duris crepitare incudibus ensis.

VIRGIL, Georgics ii, 513–531, 538–40

l. 2   *hinc:* 'from this . . .'
l. 3   *sustinere:* 'to keep, to support'   *armentum:* 'a herd'
meritus: 'well-deserving'   *iuvencus:* 'an ox'.
l. 4   *nec requies:* supply *est*   *quin . . . exuberet annus:* 'but the year overflows . . .'

l. 5   *fetus -us:* 'offspring'; but in line 9 'fruit, produce'   *Cerealis mergite culmi:* 'with sheafs of corn' (Ceres was the goddess of corn).

l. 6   *proventus -us:* 'produce'   *sulcus:* 'a furrow'   *horreum:* 'a barn'.

l. 7   *Sicyonia baca:* literally 'the Sicyonian berry' i.e. olives; Sicyon was a town famous for its olives.

trapetus: 'an oil mill' (used for pressing olives).

l. 8   *glandis:* 'an acorn'; pigs were sent out to the woods to feed on acorns in the autumn and were brought back in winter.

arbutum: wild strawberry.

l. 10   *mitis:* 'ripe'   *apricus:* 'sunny'   *vindemia:* 'grapes'.

l. 12   *ubera,* n.pl: 'udders'   *vacca:* 'a cow'.

l. 14   *luctari:* 'to struggle'   *haedus:* 'a kid'.

l. 15   *fusus:* 'stretched'.

l. 16   *ignis ubi in medio:* supply *est*   *cratera coronant:* 'fill the wine bowl'   *socii:* 'his friends'   *libare:* 'to pour a drink offering' *Lenaeus* = Bacchus, god of wine.

l. 18   *iaculum:* 'a javelin'.

l. 19   *agresti palaestra:* 'in their rustic wrestling ground'.

l. 20   *Saturnus:* Saturn, the father of Jupiter, was supposed to have lived in Italy in the Golden Age.

l. 21   *necdum:* 'not yet'   *audierant:* the subject 'they' refers to mankind as a whole   *classica* (n.pl.): war trumpet.

l. 22   *crepitare:* 'to ring out'   *incus, incudis:* 'an anvil'.

1. What is the farmer described as doing in line 1? What is the end, or purpose, of this work?
2. Why can he not rest when this work is done?
3. Which words in lines 4–6 stress the bounty of nature?
4. List the products mentioned in lines 4–10 and say with what time of year each is associated. (Virgil does not completely follow the order of the seasons; you must use your common sense as well as the text.)
5. Describe the farmer's home (ll. 11–14). What is the mood of Virgil's description, and which words especially emphasize the mood?
6. Describe how the farmer keeps festival days in as much detail as the text allows.
7. Summarize the characteristics which Virgil ascribes to the farmer's life.
8. Explain the point of line 20.
9. What is the implication of lines 21–22?

ii. The rich man

C. Plinius Fusco suo S.

Quaeris quemadmodum in Tuscis diem aetate disponam. Evigilo cum libuit, plerumque circa horam primam, saepe ante, tardius raro. Clausae fenestrae
5 manent. Cogito si quid in manibus. Notarium voco et die admisso quae formaveram dicto. Ubi hora quarta vel quinta, ut dies suasit, in xystum me vel cryptoporticum confero, reliqua meditor et dicto. Vehiculum ascendo. Ibi quoque idem quod ambulans aut iacens; durat
10 intentio mutatione ipsa refecta. Paulum redormio, dein ambulo, ungor, exerceor, lavor. Cenanti mihi, si cum uxore vel paucis, liber legitur; post cenam comoedia aut lyristes; mox cum meis ambulo, quorum in numero sunt eruditi. Ita variis sermonibus vespera extenditur, et
15 quamquam longissimus dies bene conditur. Nonnumquam ex hoc ordine aliqua mutantur. Interveniunt amici ex proximis oppidis, partemque diei ad se trahunt. Venor aliquando, sed non sine pugillaribus, ut quamvis nihil ceperim non nihil referam. Datur et colonis, ut
20 videtur ipsis, non satis temporis, quorum mihi agrestes querelae litteras nostras et haec urbana opera commendant. Vale.

PLINY, *Ep.* ix, 36

l. 2   *in Tuscis:* i.e. on his Tuscan estate in central Italy   *disponere:* 'to arrange'.

l. 3   *cum libuit:* literally 'when it has pleased (me)', i.e. 'when I like'   *plerumque:* 'usually'   *hora prima:* the first hour of the Roman day was dawn.

l. 4   *fenestrae:* here 'shutters' rather than 'windows'.

l. 5   *si quid (est) in manibus:* 'anything (i.e. any writing) I have on hand'.   *notarius:* 'secretary'.

l. 6   *formare:* 'to shape, to compose'.

l. 6   *dies:* i.e. the day's weather.

l. 7   *xystus:* 'a terrace'   *cryptoporticus:* 'a colonnade'.

l. 8   *vehiculum:* 'a carriage'   *idem:* supply *facio.*

ll. 9–10   *durat intentio . . . refecta:* 'my concentration lasts restored by . . .'

l. 11   *ungor:* 'I annoint myself'; before bathing the Romans usually rubbed themselves with olive oil.

l. 12   *comoedia:* i.e. an entertainment by a comic actor   *lyristes:* 'a lyre player'   *meis:* i.e. 'my freedmen'   *eruditus:* 'educated, learned'.

l. 15   *quamquam longissimus dies:* literally 'the day although very long' i.e. 'even the longest day'   *conditur:* 'is ended'.

l. 18   *pugillares:* 'writing tablets' (compare 11. ii).

l. 19   *colonus:* 'a tenant'.

l. 20   *non satis temporis:* this phrase is the subject of *datur.*

l. 21   *querelae:* 'complaints'.

l. 21   *litteras nostras . . . opera:* 'my literary pursuits and urbane occupations'; *urbana* involves a pun; it is contrasted with *agrestes;* 'city' and 'refined' contrasted with 'country' and 'uncouth'   *mihi commendant:* literally 'commend to me' i.e. 'make me appreciate'.

1. What question of Fuscus is Pliny answering?
2. At what time does Pliny wake up?
3. What does he do when he first wakes?
4. Describe how he spends the day after that until dinner time.
5. What diversions are provided during and after dinner?
6. What is the point of *quorum . . . eruditi* (ll. 13–14)?
7. Summarize the main features of his life *in Tuscis.*
8. List the three distractions from these pursuits.
9. Explain the meaning of *Datur . . . temporis* (ll. 19–20). What does Pliny do for his *coloni*?
10. Compare the way of life here described with that of Virgil's farmer. Which seems to you the better life? What evidence is there in this letter that Pliny found his life in the country satisfying?

iii. The town mouse and the country mouse

Olim
rusticus urbanum murem mus paupere fertur
accepisse cavo, veterem vetus hospes amicum . . .
tandem urbanus ad hunc 'Quid te iuvat' inquit, 'amice,
praerupti nemoris patientem vivere dorso?
5 vis tu homines urbemque feris praeponere silvis?
carpe viam, mihi crede, comes; terrestria quando
mortales animas vivunt sortita, neque ulla est
aut magno aut parvo leti fuga: quo, bone, circa,
dum licet, in rebus incundis vive beatus;
10 vive memor, quam sis aevi brevis.' haec ubi dicta
agrestem pepulere, domo levis exsilit; inde
ambo propositum peragunt iter, urbis aventes
moenia nocturni subrepere. iamque tenebat
nox medium caeli spatium, cum ponit uterque
15 in locuplete domo vestigia . . .
ergo ubi purpurea porrectum in veste locavit
agrestem, veluti succinctus cursitat hospes
continuatque dapes . . .
ille cubans gaudet mutata sorte bonisque
20 rebus agit laetum convivam, cum subito ingens
valvarum strepitus lectis excussit utrumque.
currere per totum pavidi conclave, magisque
exanimes trepidare, simul domus alta Molossis
personuit canibus. tum rusticus 'Haud mihi vita
25 est opus hac' ait et 'valeas: me silva cavusque
tutus ab insidiis tenui solabitur ervo.'

HORACE, *Satires* II vi, 79–117 (with omissions)

l. 1   *mus, muris:* 'a mouse'.
l. 2   *cavus:* 'a hole'.
l. 3   *quid te iuvat?:* literally 'in what way does it please you' i.e.
'what pleasure does it give you?'
l. 4   *praeruptus:* 'rugged'   *dorsum:* 'back, ridge'.
l. 5   *vis tu?:* 'won't you?'   *praeponere:* 'to prefer'.

l. 6   *comes:* literally 'as a companion' i.e. 'with me'   *quando:* 'since'   *terrestria quando . . . sortita:* literally 'since earthly creatures live having received mortal souls as their lot'.

l. 8   *leti fuga:* 'escape from death'   *quo . . . circa:* 'therefore'.

l. 10   *quam sis aevi brevis:* literally 'how you are of short life' i.e. 'how short-lived you are'.

l. 12   *propositum iter:* 'their intended journey'   *avere:* 'to be eager'.

l. 13   *nocturnus -a -um:* 'of night, by night'.

l. 13   *subrepere:* 'to creep under'.

l. 15   *locuples, locupletis:* 'rich'.

l. 16   *porrectus:* 'stretched out, reclining'   *vestis:* 'coverings'.

l. 17   *veluti . . . hospes:* 'like a girt-up (slave), his host bustles about' (a slave would pull his tunic above the knees and fix it there so that he could run freely).

l. 18   *continuatque dapes:* 'and keeps the feast going continuously' i.e. 'serves course after course'.

l. 20   *agit laetum convivam:* 'plays (the part of) the happy guest'.

l. 21   *valvarum strepitus:* 'the banging of doors'   *lectus:* 'a couch'; the Romans reclined on couches at dinner.

ll. 22–23   *currere, trepidare:* historic infinitives   *conclave, conclavis:* 'a room'.

ll. 23–24   *exanimis:* 'half-dead'   *Molossi canes:* mastiffs from Molossis (in north Greece).

l. 26   *tenui ervo:* 'with a little vetch' (a vetch is a wild bean).

1. In lines 1–2, how does Horace establish the feeling that he is describing the mice in human terms? Where else in the passage is this mood strongly established?
2. What does the town mouse ask the country mouse (ll. 3–5)? Which words show the town mouse's feelings about the country mouse's home?
3. What does the town mouse tell the country mouse to do?
4. What arguments does he give in favour of his proposal? What philosophy of life do these arguments suggest?
5. What effect do the arguments have on the country mouse?
6. When they reach the house in the city, what does the town mouse do?
7. What does the country mouse do? How does he feel?
8. What interrupts them and how do they react?
9. What conclusion does the country mouse come to?
10. What would be meant by calling this story a fable? What is its moral?

9   113

20. The gods

i. Simple piety; a farmer's prayer

Faune, Nympharum fugientum amator,
per meos fines et aprica rura
lenis incedas abeasque parvis
    aequus alumnis,
5   si tener pleno cadit haedus anno,
larga nec desunt Veneris sodali
vina craterae, vetus ara multo
    fumat odore.
ludit herboso pecus omne campo,
10   cum tibi Nonae redeunt Decembres;
festus in pratis vacat otioso
cum bove pagus;
inter audaces lupus errat agnos;
spargit agrestes tibi silva frondes;
15   gaudet invisam pepulisse fossor
    ter pede terram.

HORACE, *Odes* iii. 18

ii. A thank offering

Minervae memori Tullia Superiana, restitutione facta
sibi capillorum, V(otum) s(olvit) l(ibens) m(erito).

From Placentia in north Italy

(the last four words are, as usual, abbreviated to *v.s.l.m.*)
    Interpret this inscription, reconstructing the circumstances
in which it was set up.

114

l. 1 *Faunus:* an Italian rural deity, protector of the flocks.
l. 2 *apricus:* 'sunny'.
l. 3 *lenis:* 'gentle'.
l. 4 *aequus:* 'fair, kind'   *alumnus:* 'young creature'.
l. 5 *si:* here means 'seeing that' rather than 'if'   *pleno anno:* 'at the completion of the year' i.e. 'when the full time comes round for your festival'.
l. 6 *largus:* 'plentiful'   *sodalis:* 'companion'.
l. 7 *cratera:* wine bowl.
l. 8 *odor:* 'incense'.
l. 11 *vacare:* 'to be at leisure, to keep holiday'.
l. 12 *pagus:* 'village'.
l. 15 *fossor:* 'a ditcher'   *pepulisse:* literally: 'to have struck' (*pellere*).

1. For what does the farmer pray?
2. What does *cadit* (l. 5) mean here? What three offerings to Faunus are listed in this stanza?
3. When was the festival held? What other indication of the season do you find in the poem?
4. Line 13. What is said here is obviously untrue; why should Horace say this? Where do you find a similar idea in the Old Testament?
5. What is the ditcher doing? Why is the earth described as *invisam* (l. 15)?
6. Write in the greatest possible detail a description of the festival of Faunus, based on this passage.

l. 1 *memor:* 'remembering' i.e. Minerva did not forget Tullia.
l. 2 *capilli:* 'hair'.
l. 2 *merito:* 'deservedly' i.e. Minerva earned the offering.

iii. Scepticism: religion overthrown by science

In his poem *De rerum natura*, Lucretius expounds the teaching of the Greek philosopher Epicurus. Epicurus, following the atomic theory of earlier Greek scientists, explained the phenomena of the universe entirely in terms of natural causation; the possibility of divine intervention in human affairs was rejected.

Humana ante oculos foede cum vita iaceret
in terris oppressa gravi sub religione,
quae caput a caeli regionibus ostendebat
horribili super aspectu mortalibus instans,
5 primum Graius homo mortales tollere contra
est oculos ausus primusque obsistere contra;
quem neque fama deum nec fulmina nec minitanti
murmure compressit caelum, sed eo magis acrem
irritat animi virtutem, effringere ut arta
10 naturae primus portarum claustra cupiret.
ergo vivida vis animi pervicit, et extra
processit longe flammantia moenia mundi
atque omne immensum peragravit mente animoque,
unde refert nobis victor quid possit oriri,
15 quid nequeat, finita potestas denique cuique
quanam sit ratione atque alte terminus haerens.
quare religio pedibus subiecta vicissim
obteritur, nos exaequat victoria caelo.

LUCRETIUS i, 62–79

l. 1 *ante oculos:* 'before (men's) eyes', i.e. 'in the sight of all'.
l. 2 *in terris:* 'on the ground'.
l. 4 *super* (adv.) = *desuper*, 'from above'   *mortalibus:* 'mortal men'; but in line 5 *mortales* is an adjective agreeing with *oculos*.
l. 5 *contra* is here and in line 6 used as an adverb.
l. 6 *obsistere:* 'to withstand, to stand up against'.
l. 7 *fama deum:* 'stories about the gods'   *minitari:* 'to threaten'.
l. 8 *eo magis:* literally 'by so much the more', i.e. 'all the more'.

l. 9 *irritat:* 'it (i.e. *fama deum* etc.) provoked' *effringere:* 'to break' *artus:* 'narrow, cramping'.

l. 10 *claustra* (n.pl.): 'bars, bounds' *cupiret = cuperet.*

ll. 11–12 *extra . . . mundi:* 'he advanced far beyond (*longe extra*) the flaming walls of the world'; Epicurus believed the world (*mundus*, including the sun, moon and stars) to be spherical and surrounded by a belt of flame.

l. 13 *omne:* 'the universe'; the word is used as a noun; the universe is infinite (*immensum*) and contains countless other worlds. *peragrare:* 'to travel through'.

l. 14 *referre:* 'to bring back (word), to report'.

l. 15 *nequeo:* 'I cannot' *finita . . . haerens:* 'finally (*denique*), how (*quanam ratione*) there is for each thing a limited power and a deep set (*alte haerens*) boundary stone' i.e. the powers and potentialities of everything in the universe are limited and intelligible; therefore, nothing is illimitable, unintelligible or supernatural.

l. 17 *vicissim:* 'in its turn'.

l. 18 *obterere:* 'to crush, trample down' *exaequare:* 'to make equal, to place on a level with'.

1. What picture is presented by lines 1–4?
2. What did Epicurus (*Graius homo*) do, according to Lucretius (ll. 5–6)?
3. Explain the significance of *fama, fulmina, minitanti murmure* (l. 7).
4. What picture is presented by *effringere . . . claustra* (ll. 9–10)?
5. *pervicit* (l. 11): what victory is referred to? Explain it (a) in terms of Lucretius' imagery (picture language) (b) in literal terms.
6. What message did Epicurus bring back from his journey of the mind? Explain what Lucretius says in lines 14–16 and summarize it in modern terms.
7. What, according to Lucretius, was the effect of Epicurus' victory on religion?
8. Summarize what Lucretius says in this passage in simple terms.
9. Epicurus preached calm and freedom from violent emotion; does this passage seem to you consistent in spirit with this teaching?
10. Where in the passage does Lucretius use alliteration (repetition of consonants) and assonance (repetition of vowel sounds), and to what effect?

iv. The universal law of God

The thought expressed in this passage is Stoic. The founder of the Stoic school was a Cypriot, Zeno, who taught in Athens about 300 B.C. The views of Zeno were opposed on most points to those of his contemporary Epicurus (compare 21, i and ii). Stoic teaching was widely accepted by the educated Romans and had considerable influence on Christian doctrine.

Est quidem vera lex recta ratio naturae congruens, diffusa in omnes, constans, sempiterna, quae vocat ad officium iubendo, vetando a fraude deterreat; quae tamen neque probos frustra iubet aut vetat, nec impro-
5 bos iubendo aut vetando movet. Huic legi nec obrogari fas est neque derogari ex hac aliquid licet neque tota abrogari potest, nec vero aut per senatum aut per populum solvi hac lege possumus, neque est quaerendus explanator aut interpres eius alius, nec erit alia lex
10 Romae, alia Athenis, alia nunc, alia posthac, sed et omnes gentes et omni tempore una lex et sempiterna et immutabilis continebit, unusque erit quasi magister et imperator omnium deus, ille legis inventor, disceptator, lator; cui qui non parebit, ipse se fugiet ac naturam
15 hominis aspernatus hoc ipso luet maximas poenas, etiamsi cetera supplicia, quae putantur, effugerit.

CICERO, *de Republi* III

l. 1 *recta ratio naturae congruens:* 'right reason in harmony with nature'.

l. 3 *fraus, fraudis:* 'wrong'.

ll. 5–7 *obrogare:* 'to propose a new law in place of an old one, to replace'; *derogare:* 'to modify': *abrogare:* 'to annul'; all three are technical legal terms.

l. 8 *solvere:* 'to exempt from (a law)'.

l. 9 *explanator:* 'interpreter'.

ll. 13–14 *magister et imperator:* 'general and supreme commander'.

l. 13 *disceptator:* 'arbitrator' *lator:* 'proposer, promulgator'.

l. 14 *cui:* 'and he who does not obey it' (or 'him'); *cui* may refer to God but more probably refers to the law.

ll. 14–15 *ipse se fugiet:* 'will be trying to escape from himself' *aspernari:* 'to spurn, to reject'.

ll. 15–16 *luere:* 'to pay' *cetera supplicia, quae putantur:* 'other punishments, which are thought (to exist)'.

1. Considering lines 1–5, can you find one English word which corresponds fairly closely to what Cicero appears to mean by *vera lex?* How is Cicero's *vera lex* like and unlike the English equivalent?

2. Summarize briefly the meaning of *Huic legi* (l. 5) to *lator* (l. 14).

3. Explain the meaning of the last sentence. To what does *hoc ipso* refer?

4. What do you suppose is meant by *cetera supplicia, quae putantur* (l. 16)?

5. In what important respects do the views implied in this passage differ from the beliefs of popular Roman religion?

6. Is any of the views expressed in the passage irreconcilable with Christian teaching? Which seem to be most clearly reflected in Christian doctrine?

7. What is the tone of this passage? How does the language used help to express the tone?

21. Death

i. An Epicurean's view

The scene of this extract is a funeral; the mourners stand beside the dead man's pyre and address him. Lucretius answers what they say.

'iam iam non domus accipiet te laeta neque uxor
optima nec dulces occurrent oscula nati
praeripere et tacita pectus dulcedine tangent.
non poteris factis florentibus esse tuisque
5 praesidium. misero misere' aiunt 'omnia ademit
una dies infesta tibi tot praemia vitae.'
illud in his rebus non addunt 'nec tibi earum
iam desiderium rerum super insidet una.'
quod bene si videant animo dictisque sequantur,
10 dissolvant animi magno se angore metuque.
'tu quidem ut es leto sopitus, sic eris aevi
quod superest cunctis privatu' doloribus aegris.
at nos horrifico cinefactum te prope busto
insatiabiliter deflevimus, aeternumque
15 nulla dies nobis maerorem e pectore demet.'
illud ab hoc igitur quaerendum est, quid sit amari
tanto opere, ad somnum si res redit atque quietem,
cur quisquam aeterno possit tabescere luctu.

LUCRETIUS iii, 894–911

---

l. 1 *iam iam non:* 'now no more'.
l. 2 *nati:* 'children'   *oscula . . . praeripere:* 'to snatch the first kisses' (the infinitive expresses purpose).
l. 4 *factis florentibus esse:* literally 'to be (a man) of flourishing deeds', i.e. 'to be successful'.
l. 5 *adimere:* 'to take away'.
l. 6 *infestus:* 'hateful'.
l. 8 *desiderium:* 'desire for what is lost, yearning'.

ll. 7–8   *tibi . . . super insidet una:* 'will remain with (*una*) you any more (*super*)': *una* and *super* are adverbs; *insidet* is from *insido, insidere* = 'to be seated on, to be fixed on'.

l. 10   *dissolvere:* 'to free'   *animi:* genitive with *angore* 'from anxiety of mind'.

l. 11   *letum:* 'death'   *sopire:* 'to put to sleep'.

ll. 11–12   *aevi quod superest:* literally 'for what of time is left', i.e. 'for all time to come'   *cunctus:* 'all'   *privatu* = *privatus*, 'deprived of, freed from'.

l. 13   *cinefactus:* 'turned to ashes'   *bustum:* 'a funeral pyre'.

l. 14   *insatiabiliter:* 'insatiably, unconsolably'.

l. 15   *maeror:* 'grief'   *demere:* 'to take away'.

l. 16   *ab hoc:* 'from this man', i.e. from the man who speaks the lines above   *quid sit amari tanto opere:* literally 'what there is so exceedingly of bitterness'.

l. 18   *tabescere:* 'to waste away'   *cur*, 'why', here means 'because of which . . .'

1. What picture is painted in the first three lines? Explain the phrase *tacita dulcedine.*
2. Lines 5–6. (a) explain the grammar of the words *misero misere.* Why are they placed in this position? (b) With which words do *omnia, una, infesta* agree? (c) Suggest what Lucretius means by *praemia vitae.*
3. What do the mourners omit to add (ll. 7–8)?
4. Explain what lines 9–10 mean. In particular, explain the significance of *angor* and *metus.*
5. Summarize briefly the sense of lines 11–16. How do these lines represent a change of attitude on the part of the mourners?
6. Lines 13–15. *At nos:* with which word is *nos* contrasted? Which words in these lines build up and emphasize the feelings of the mourners? How does the rhythm of line 14 help to express these feelings?
7. What is Lucretius' final question?
8. Summarize the argument Lucretius gives in this passage in brief and unemotional form. Do you find his argument convincing?
9. Your answer to question 8 will be quite 'unpoetic'; what, apart from versification, gives the passage its poetic quality?
10. What do you suppose is Lucretius' purpose in this passage?

ii. A Stoic view

Virgil has been describing the remarkable social and political virtues of the society of the bees.

His quidam signis atque haec exempla secuti
esse apibus partem divinae mentis et haustus
aetherios dixere; deum namque ire per omnes
terrasque tractusque maris caelumque profundum;
5 hinc pecudes, armenta, viros, genus omne ferarum,
quemque sibi tenues nascentem arcessere vitas:
scilicet huc reddi deinde ac resoluta referri
omnia, nec morti esse locum, sed viva volari
sideris in numerum atque alto succedere caelo.

VIRGIL, Georgics iv, 219–227

iii. Pagan nihilism

Dis manibus sacrum. Aureliae Vercellae coniugi dulcissimae, quae vixit plus minus annis XVII. 'Non fui, fui, non sum, non desidero.' Anthimus maritus eius.

Dessau 8162

What does this epitaph tell you about the beliefs of Anthimus?

iv. Christian conviction

Aureliae Mariae puellae, virgini innocentissimae, sancte pergenti ad iustos et electos in pace. Quae vixit annos XVII, menses V, dies XVIIII, sponsata Aurelio Damati diebus XXV. Aurelius Ianisireius veteranus et
5 Sextilia parentes infelicissimae filiae dulcissimae ac amantissimae contra votum. Qui dum vivent, habent magnum dolorem. Martyres sancti, in mente habete Mariam.

Epitaph from Aquileia in Italy

l. 1 *quidam:* subject of *dixere*   *his signis atque haec exempla secuti:* literally 'because of these signs and following these examples (i.e. this evidence)'.

l. 2 *apis:* 'a bee'   *haustus aetherios:* 'draughts of ether'; *aether*, according to the Stoics, was a light and fiery element surrounding and permeating the universe; it was the source of all life and intelligence and was sometimes called the soul of the universe (*anima mundi*).

l. 4 *tractus maris:* 'the expanses of the sea'.

l. 5 *hinc:* 'from this', i.e. from god.

l. 6 *tenuis:* 'fine, subtle'.

l. 7 *scilicet:* 'surely'   *huc:* 'to this', i.e. to god   *resolutus:* 'dissolved'.

1. What conclusion do some people draw from the behaviour of the bees?
2. How do they account for what they say?
3. What happens, on this theory, when a creature is born?
4. What happens when it dies?
5. Explain the meaning of *sed viva . . . caelo* (ll. 8–9).
6. *nec morti esse locum* (l. 8): does the theory allow for the possibility of individual survival after death?

l. 2 *pergere:* 'to go'   *electus:* 'chosen'.

l. 3 *sponsatus:* 'betrothed'.

l. 4 *veteranus:* a retired soldier.

l. 6 *contra votum:* this appears to mean 'contrary to their prayers'. Supply here e.g. 'made this memorial'.

1. Summarize the information this epitaph gives about Maria and her parents.
2. Assemble all the evidence given in the epitaph that Maria was a Christian and explain the relevant phrases.
3. Where is the Christian conviction in life after death made plain? Do you find the phrases *infelicissimae filiae* (l. 5) and *habent magnum dolorem* (l. 7) consistent with this conviction?

Vocabulary

1. All vowels long by nature are marked thus: vīs, except for final -o and -i, which are always long unless marked short, e.g. modŏ. Except for diphthongs and final -o and -i, all unmarked vowels are short by nature.

2. Some very common words are omitted from the vocabulary. Words and phrases occurring once only and explained in the notes are omitted from the vocabulary.

abdo, abdere, abdidi, abditum: I hide
abeo, abīre, abii, abitum: I go away
abicio, abicere, abiēci, abiĕctum: I throw away, throw down
absentia, -ae, f.: absence
abstuli: see aufero
absum, abesse, āfui: I am absent, I am away
absūmo, -ere, absūmi, absūmptum: I use up, take up
ac: and
accēdo, -ere, accessi, accessum: I approach
accendo, -ere, accendi, accēnsum: I set on fire, I fire, rouse
ācer, ācris, ācre: keen, spirited
accidit, accidere, accidit: it happens
accipio, accipere, accēpi, accĕptum: I receive, accept, I hear
accūso (1): I accuse
acquiēsco, acquiēscere: I rest on; I find pleasure in
acūtus -a -um: sharp, clever
addo, -ere, addidi, additum: I add
addūco, -ere, addūxi, adductum: I lead to; I induce
adfero, adferre, attuli, adlātum: I bring to, I report
adficio, adficere, adfēci, adfectum: I affect
adhuc: still
adicio, adicere, adiēci, adiectum: I add
adiuvo, -āre, adiūvi, adiūtum: I help
admīror (1): I admire, wonder at
admitto, -ere, admīsi, admissum: I let in, admit
admoveo, -ēre, admōvi, admōtum: I move towards
adprobo (1): I approve
adquiēsco = acquiēsco
adsedeo, -ēre, adsēdi, adsessum: I sit down
adsentior, -īri, adsēnsus: I agree with (+ dative)
adsto, adstāre, adstiti: I stand beside
adsum, adesse, adfui: I am present, I am here
adulēscentia, -ae: youth
advenio, -īre, advēni, adventum: I arrive
adversus, -a -um: facing, opposed
adversus (prep. with acc.): opposite, against

aedēs, aedis, f.: a temple; plural, a house
aedifico (1): I build
aeger, aegra, aegrum: sick; adv. aegre: scarcely, with difficulty
aequālitās, -ātis, f.: equality, evenness, smoothness
aequus -a, -um: equal, level, fair
āēr, āēris, n.: air
aestās, aestātis, f.: summer
aetās, aetātis, f.: age, life
aeternus -a -um: eternal
aevum -i: age, time
affero = adfero
agellus -i: a little field, little farm
ager, agri, m.: a field, farm
agitātio, -iōnis, f.: movement
agitātor, -ōris, m.: a driver
agito (1); I move, I spend (time)
agmen, agminis, n.: a column, row
agnus, -i, m.: a lamb
ago, agere, ēgi, āctum: I do, I discuss, I spend (time); age (imp.):
    come on
agrestis -e: country, rustic
aio: I say
aliēnus -a -um: belonging to another, foreign
aliquando: at some time
aliquis, aliquid: someone, something
alternus -a -um: alternate
altus -a -um: deep, high; altum (neuter): the deep (sea)
alumnus, -i, m.: foster child
amāns, amantis, c.: a lover
amātor, -ōris, m.: a lover
ambo, ambōrum: both
ambulo (1): I walk
amīca, -ae, f.: a girl friend
amīcus, -i, m.: a friend
amīcitia, -ae, f.: friendship
āmitto, -ere, amīsi, amissum: I let slip, lose
amor, amōris, m.: love
amplius (comparative adv.): more
angustus -a -um: narrow
anima, -ae, f.: soul, spirit
animadverto, -ere, -verti, -versum: I notice
animus, -i, m.: mind, courage, spirit
antecessor, -oris: predecessor
antehāc: before this, formerly
antīquus -a -um: old
appello (1): I call (by name)
aper, apri, m.: a boar

126

aperio, -īre, aperui, apertum: I open, reveal
apertus -a -um: open; adv. aperte
appāreo, -ēre, appārui: I appear
apto (1): I fit, get ready
apud (prep. with acc.): at, among, to
aqua, -ae, f.: water
āra, -ae, f.: altar
arātrum, -i, n.: a plough
arbitror (1): I think
argentum, -i, n.: silver
armentum, -i, n.: flock, herd
arcesso, -ere, accessīvi, accessītum: I summon
ārdeo, -ēre, ārsi: I am on fire, burn
ars, artis, f.: skill, art
arx, arcis, f.: a citadel, a summit
ascendo, -ere, ascendi, ascēnsum: I climb, mount, board
aspectus, -ūs, m.: a look
asper, aspera, asperum: rough
assequor, -i, assecūtus: I follow after, I reach, achieve
at: but
atque: and
atrōx, atrōcis: savage, atrocious
attollo, -ere: I raise
auctio, -iōnis, f.: auction
auctor, -ōris, m.: an adviser, author, authority; auctore me: on my
    advice
auctōritās, -ātis, f.: authority
audācia, -ae, f.: boldness, recklessness
audāx, audācis: bold, reckless
audeo, -ēre, ausus: I dare
audio (4): I hear
audītor, -ōris, m.: a hearer, listener
aufero, auferre, abstuli, ablātum: I carry away
augeo, -ēre, auxi, auctum: I increase
aura, -ae, f.: a breeze
aureus, -a -um: golden
aurum, -i, n.: gold
avītus -a -um: belonging to one's grandfather, ancestral
āvius -a -um: trackless
āvoco (1): I call away
avus, -i, m.: grandfather

balneum, -i, n.: bath, bathroom
beātus -a -um: blessed, happy
beneficium, -i, n.: kindness
bīlis, bīlis, m.: bile
bos, bovis, c.: ox, cow

cado, -ere, cecĭdi, cāsum: I fall, fall out, end
caecus -a -um: blind
caedes, caedis, f.: slaughter, murder
caedo, -ere, cecīdi, caesum: I strike, beat, kill
caelum, -i, n.: heaven, sky, climate
calidus -a -um: warm
campus, -i, m.: plain, field
capillus, -i, m.: hair
captīvus, -i, m.: captive
caput, capitis, n.: head; a person; e.g. invīsum caput = hated man
carcer, carceris, m.: an enclosed space; a prison; the starting gate on
   a race track
cāritās, -tātis, f.: dearness, affection
carmen, carminis, n.: a song
carpo, -ere, carpsi: I pluck, take
cārus -a -um: dear, beloved
castīgo (1): I rebuke, castigate
castra, castrōrum, n.pl.: a camp
castus -a -um: pure, chaste
cāsus, -ūs, m.: a fall, chance, misfortune
caterva, -ae, f.: a band of people
causa, -ae, f.: a cause, reason: causā: for the sake of
cautus -a -um: careful, cautious
cēdo, -ere, cessi, cessum: I yield, give way, retire
celebro (1): I celebrate, make famous
celer, celeris, celere: quick
celero (1): I speed up, hasten
cēna, -ae, f.: dinner
cēnātus -a -um: having dined
cēno (1): I dine
cēnseo, cēnsēre, cēnsui: I give an opinion, vote
cerno, -ere, crēvi, crētum: I see
certāmen, -minis, n.: a contest, struggle
certē: certainly
cervix, cervīcis, f.: neck
cesso (1): I am idle
cēteri -ae -a: the rest
cēterum (adv.): but
chīrugus, -i, m.: a surgeon
cinis, cineris, m.: ash
circā (prep. with acc.): around, about (of time and place)
circēnsis -e: of the circus
circum = circā
circumseco (1): I cut round
circumsisto, -ere, -stiti: I stand round
cīvitās, -tātis, f.: a state
clam: secretly

clāmo (1): I shout
clāmor, -ōris, m.: a shout
clārus -a -um: bright, light, famous
classis, classis, f.: a fleet
claudo, -ere, clausi, clausum: I shut
clēmenter: mercifully, kindly
coepi, coepisse: I began
cogitātio, -iōnis, f.: thought
cogito (1): I think, ponder
cognōsco, -ere, -nōvi, -nitum: I get to know, learn: cognovi: I know
cōgo, -ere, coēgi, coāctum: I collect, I compel
cohors, cohortis, f.: a cohort
colligo, -ere, collēgi, collēctum: I gather, collect
collis, collis, m.: a hill
colloco (1): I place, I spend
collum, -i, n.: neck
colo, -ere, colui, cultum: I till, I inhabit, I respect
commendātio, -iōnis, f.: recommendation
commendo (1): I recommend
comes, comitis, c.: companion
cōmis -e: affable, friendly; adv. comiter
committo, -ere, -mīsi, -missum: I commit, I entrust, I engage (in
    battle)
commoror (1): I delay, stay
commoveo, -ēre, -mōvi, -mōtum: I move (literally, and of feelings)
commūnis -e: shared, common
complūres -a: several, a good many
comparo (1): I obtain, I compare
comprehendo, -ere, -prehendi, -hēnsum: I seize, arrest
comprimo, -ere, -pressi, -pressum: I suppress
concieo, -ēre, concīvi, concitum: I stir up
concubīna, -ae, f.: a concubine
concupio, -cupere, -cupīvi, -cupitum: I desire, long for
concupisco, -cupiscere: I long for
condo, -ere, condidi, conditum: I gather, I hide, I found
cōnfero, -ferre, -tuli, -lātum: I bring together, I collect, I compare;
    me confero: I take myself, I go
cōnficio, -ficere, -fēci, -fectum: I finish
cōnfīdo, -ere, -fīsus: I trust in, confide in
cōnfirmo, (1): I strengthen, encourage
cōnfiteor, -ēri, -fessus: I confess
cōnfluo, -ere, -fluxi: I flock together
conicio, conicere, coniēci, coniĕctum: I throw, I hurl
coniūnx, coniugis, c.: a wife or husband
conloco = colloco
conor (1): I try
cōnscius -a -um: knowing, conscious of; an accomplice

cōnsēnsus, -us, m.: agreement
cōnservus, -i, m.: a fellow slave
cōnsidero (1): I consider
cōnsilium, -i, n.: a plan, policy
cōnsisto, -ere, -stiti: I halt, stand still
cōnspicio, -spicere, -spexi, -spectum: I catch sight of
cōnstans, cōnstantis: constant, unchanging
cōnsuētūdo, -tudinis, f.: custom
cōnsulāris, -is, m.: a man of consular rank, i.e. an ex-consul
cōnsulo, -ere, -sului, -sultum: I make plans
cōnsulto (1): I consult
contemno, -ere, -tempsi, -temptum: I despise
contemptus, -ūs, m .: contempt
contendo, -ere, -tendi, -tentum: I try vigorously; I struggle, fight;
    I demand
contineo, -ēre, -tinui, -tentum: I hold, embrace
contingit, contingere, contigit: it happens
contrā (prep. with acc.): opposite, against
contrā (adv.): on the other hand, the opposite
convalēsco, -ere: I get well, convalesce
convoco (1): I call together
coquo, -ere: I cook, ripen
cornū, -ūs, n.: horn
corpus, corporis, n.: body
corrumpo, -ere, -rūpi, -ruptum: I spoil, corrupt
cotidiē: daily, every day
cratēra, -ae, f.: a wine bowl
crēdībilis -e: credible
crēdo, -ere, crēdidi, crēditum: I believe, trust (with dative of
person)
crēsco, -ere, crēvi, crētum: I grow
crīmen, crīminis, n.: a charge, a reproach, a crime
cruentus -a -um: bloody
cruor, cruōris, m.: blood, gore
cubo, -āre, cubui, cubitum: I lie down
culpo (1): I blame
cunctor (1): I delay, hesitate
cupiditās, -tātis, f.: greed, desire
cupidus -a -um: desirous, eager
cupio, cupere, cupīvi, cupitum: I desire
cūra, -ae, f.: care
cūria, -ae, f.: the senate house
cūro (1): I care for, look after
curro, -ere, cucurri, cursum: I run
currus, -ūs, m.: a chariot
cursus, -ūs, m.: a running, a race, a course, a voyage
custōdia, -ae, f.: custody

custōdio (4): I guard
custōs, custōdis, m.: a guard

dēbeo (2): I owe, I ought
dēcēdo, -ere, -cessi, -cessum: I depart, I die
dēcerno, -ere, -crēvi, -crētum: I decide, I vote
decet, decēre, decuit: it suits, it is right for (impersonal verb with
   accusative of person)
dēcrētum, -i, n.: a decree
dēcurro, -ere, -curri, -cursum: I run down
decus, decoris, n.: honour, virtue, grace
dēditio, -iōnis, f.: surrender
dēdūco, -ere, -duxi, -ductum: I lead down, I launch (of ships)
dēfendo, -ere, -fendi, -fēnsum: I defend
dēfleo, -ēre, -flēvi, -flētum: I weep over, mourn
dēicio, dēicere, dēiēci, dēiectum: I throw down
dein: next, then
deinde: next, then
dēlecto (1): I please, delight
dēlectus, -ūs, m.: levy, conscription
dēmitto, -ere, -mīsi, -missum: I send down, let hang
dēmo, -ere, dēmi, dēmptum: I take away
dēmum: at last
dēnsus -a -um: thick, dense
dēporto (1): carry (down)
dēprecor (1): I pray (against something)
dērigo, -ere, -rēxi, -rēctum: I direct
dēscendo, -ere, -scendi, -sēnsum: I descend
dēsero, -ere, -serui, sertum: I desert
dēsīderium, -i, n.: longing, desire
dēsīdero (1): I long for, miss, desire
dēsum, dēesse, dēfui: I fail, I am wanting
dēterreo (2): I frighten off, deter
deus, -i, m.: a god; dis manibus: to the departed spirits
dēveho, -ere, -vēxi, -vectum: I carry down
dēvinco, -ere, -vīci, -victum: I defeat, I subdue
dexter, dextra, dextrum: right, dextra (manus): right hand
dicio, diciōnis: sway, power
dicto (1): I dictate
dictum, -i, n.: a saying, a word
didūco, -ere, -duxi, ductum: I draw apart, I divide
diffugio, -fugere, fūgi: I flee away
diffundo, -ere, -fūdi, -fūsum: I pour out, I disperse, diffuse
digitus, -i, m.: a finger
dignitās, -ātis, f.: worth, rank
dignus -a -um: worthy, worthy of (with abl.)
dīligēns, diligentis: careful, conscientious

dīligentia, -ae, f.: care
dīligo, -ere, -lēgi, -lēctum: I love
dīmitto, -ere, -mīsi, -missum: I send away, dismiss
dīmoveo, -ēre, -mōvi, -mōtum: I move apart
discēdo, -ere, -cessi, -cessum: I depart, I abandon
discerno, -ere, -crēvi, -crētum: I distinguish, I discern
discipulus, -i, m.: pupil
disco, -ere, didici: I learn
discolor, discolōris: variegated, of different colours
discrīmen, discrīminis, n.: crisis
discutio, -cutere: I shake off
dispōno, -ere, -posui, -positum: I arrange
dissolvo, -ere, -solvi, -solūtum: I dissolve, free
distraho, -ere, -trāxi, -tractum: I drag apart
dītissimus -a -um: richest, very rich
diū: for a long time, comparative: diutius
dīversus -a -um: different
dīves, dīvitis: rich
dīvīnus -a -um: divine
doceo, -ēre, docui, doctum: I teach
doctor, doctōris, m.: teacher
doleo (2): I feel pain, I grieve, grieve for
dolor, dolōris, m.: pain, grief, anxiety
domina, -ae, f.: mistress
dominicus -a -um: belonging to the master
domus, domūs, f.: home, house: domi, at home
donec: until
dōno (1): I give, present
dormio (4): I sleep
dubius -a -um: doubtful: sine dubio: without doubt
dulcēdo, -inis, f.: sweetness
dulcis -e: sweet
dum: while, until
dux, ducis, c: leader, guide

ecce: see! behold!
ēdo, ēdere, ēdidi, ēditum: I give
ēdūco, -ere, edūxi, eductum: I lead out
ēdūco (1); I educate
efferre, efferrre, extuli, ēlātum: I carry out
effugio, effugere, efūgi: I flee away, escape
effundo, -ere, effūdi, effūsum: I pour out
ēgredior, egredi, egressus: I come out
ēicio, ēicere, ēiēci, ēiectum: I throw out
ēlectus -a -um: chosen
ēlegāns, elegantis: elegant
ēligo, -ere, ēlegi, ēlectum: I choose

ēloquentia, -ae, f.: eloquence, rhetorical skill
ēmendo (1): I emend, correct
ēmitto, -ere, ēmīsi, ēmissum: I send out
ēmo, -ere, ēmi, ēmptum: I buy
ēmollio (4): I soften
ēnoto (1): I note down
ēnsis, ēnsis, m.: a sword
ēnuntio (1): I announce, make public
eo (adv.): thither, to that place, to that point
epistula, -ae, f.: a letter
eques, equitis, c.: a horseman; a knight
ergā (prep. with acc.): towards
ergo: therefore, and so
ēripio, ēripere, ēripui, ēreptum: I snatch away, I rescue
erro (1): I wander, I am lost, I am wrong
ērudio (4): I train, educate
ērudītus -a -um: learned
etiam: even, also; yes; etiam atque etiam: again and again
etsi: even if, although
ēvādo, -ere, ēvāsi, ēvāsum: I escape, get away from
ēvenio, -īre, ēvēni, ēventum: I come out; evenit: it turns out, happens
ēvigilo (1): I wake up
ēvolo (1): I fly away
excēdo, -ere, -cessi, -cessum: I go out from, I leave
excipio, -cipere, -cēpi, -ceptum: I receive
excito (1): I rouse, excite
exclāmo (1): I shout out
excutio, -cutere, -cussi, -cussum: I shake off
exemplum, -i, n.: an example
exeo, exīre, exii, exitum: I go out
exerceo (2): I exercise
exhortātio, -iōnis, f.: exhortation, encouragement
exilium, -i, n.: exile
exīstimo (1): I think
exitus, -ūs, m.: a way out, outcome, end
exorior, -orīri, -ortus: I rise out, arise
experior, -perīri, -pertus: I try, I test, I find by experience
expōno, -ere, -posui, -positum: I put out, expose
exseco, -āre, -secui, -sectum: I cut out
exsectio, -iōnis, f.: a cutting out
exsilio, -silere, -silui: I jump out
exspecto (1): I wait for, I wait
espīro (1): I breathe out, I expire
exstinguo, -ere, exstīnxi, exstīnctum: I put out, extinguish, destroy
exstruo, -ere, -struxi, -structum: I build
extendo, -ere, -tendi, -tentum: I stretch out

externus -a -um: foreign
exterritus -a -um: terrified
extraho, -ere, -trāxi, -tractum: I drag out, draw out
exuo, -ere, exui, exūtum: I take off

fābula, -ae, f.: a story, fiction
facētiae, -ārum, f.: wit
facinus, facinōris, n.: a deed, crime
factum, -i, n.: a deed, a fact
fallo, -ere, fefelli, falsum: I deceive, elude
fāma, -ae, f.: rumour, reputation
fames, famis, f.: hunger
familiāris, -is, c.: a friend
fās, n. (indecl. noun): morally right
fātum, -i, n.: fate
faveo, -ēre, fāvi, fautum: I favour, support
favor, favōris, m.: favour, support
fēlīx, fēlīcis: fortunate, lucky
fera, -ae, f.: a wild beast
ferē: almost, about
fero, ferre, tuli, lātum: I carry, bear, undergo, put up with:
    ferunt: men say, fertur: is said
ferōcia, -ae, f.: fierceness, ferocity
ferrum, -i, n.: iron, sword
ferus -a -um: wild, savage
fessus -a -um: tired
festīno (1): I hasten
festus -a -um: festival
fidēs, fidēi, f.: loyalty, trust, protection
fīdus -a -um: faithful, loyal
fīlia, -ae, f.: a daughter
fingo, -ere, finxi, fictum: I make up, compose
fīnis, fīnis, m.: end, finish; fīnēs (pl.): boundaries, territory
fīnitimus, -a -um: neighbouring
flāmen, flāminis, m.: a priest
flecto, -ere, flexi, flectum: I bend, I turn
flōreo (2): I flower, flourish
flōs, flōris; m.: flower
flūctus, -ūs, m.: a wave
fluo, fluere, flūxi: I flow
foedus -a -um: foul, base, disgraced
foedus, foederis, n.: a treaty
for, fāri, fātus: I say, speak
forma, -ae, f.: shape, figure, beauty
formīdo, formīdinis, f.: fear, nervousness
formo (1): I shape, compose
fortasse: perhaps

forte: by chance
fortūna, -ae, f.: fortune
fortūnātus -a -um: blessed by fortune, lucky
forum, -i, n.: a city centre (especially of the *forum* at Rome)
frango, -ere, frēgi, frāctum: I break
frequēns, frequentis: frequent
frīgus, frīgoris, n.: cold
frōns, frondis, m.: a leaf
frōns, frontis, f.: front
frūctus, -ūs, m.: fruit, profit
fruges, frugum, f.: fruit, harvest
fruor, frui, frūctus/fruitus: I enjoy (with abl.)
frūstrā: in vain
fuga, -ae, f.: flight, escape
fulmen, fulminis, n.: a thunderbolt
fulvus -a -um: tawny, yellowy brown
fūmo (1): I smoke
furo, -ere: I rage
furor, furōris, m.: rage, fury, madness

gaudeo, -ēre, gavīsus: I rejoice
gelidus -a -um: cold
gēns, gentis, f.: a people, a nation
genus, generis, n.: a family, a race, a kind
gladius, -i, m.: a sword
glōria, -ae, f.: glory
gradus, -ūs, m.: a step
Graius -a -um: Greek
grāmen, grāminis, n.: grass
grandis -e: big
grātia, -ae, f.: gratitude, favour, influence: grātiae (pl.): thanks;
    grātias agere: to thank
grātus -a -um: pleasing, grateful
gravis -e: heavy, serious, reliable; adv. grave or graviter
gressus, -ūs, m.: a step
gubernāculum, -i, n.: rudder, tiller
gubernātor, ōris, m.: helmsman
gusto (1): I taste

habito (1): I live in, inhabit
haedus, -i, m.: a kid, a young goat
haud: not
herba, -ae, f.: grass
herbōsus -a -um: grassy
heri: yesterday
hic (adv.): here; hinc: from here
hicce = hic

135

hiems, hiemis, f.: winter, a storm
hodiē: to-day
hodiernus -a -um: of to-day
homicīdium, -i, n.: murder, homicide
honestus -a -um: honourable
horribilis -e: terrifying
horrificus -a -um: horrifyng
hortor (1): I encourage
hortus, -i, m.: garden
hospes, hospitis, c.: a host, or guest; a friend
hostis, hostis, m.: an enemy
hūc: hither; hūc . . . illūc . . .: hither and thither, this way and that
humānitās, -ātis, f.: kindness, consideration, humanity
humānus -a -um: kind, considerate
humilis -e: humble, lowly

iaceo (2): I lie
iacio, iacere, iēci, iactum: I throw
iacto (1): I throw about, toss: me iacto: I boast
ignāvus -a -um: cowardly, idle
ignis, ignis, m.: fire
ignōsco, -ere, ignōvi, ignōtum: I pardon (with dative)
ignōtus -a -um: unknown
illūc: thither, to that place
illustris -e: bright, famous, illustrious
imitor (1): I imitate
imminēns, imminentis: overhanging, threatening, imminent
immōbilis -e: motionless, immobile
immūtābilis -e: unchanging, immutable
impedio (4): I hinder, prevent
impendo, -ere, impendi, impēnsum: I spend
imperito (1): I rule, govern
imperium, -i, n.: an order, command, empire
impero (1): I order (with dative)
impetus, -ūs, m.: charge, attack
impiger, impigra, impigrum: energetic
impius -a -um: wicked, impious
improbus -a -um: wicked, bad
incautus -a -um: incautious, off one's guard
incēdo, -ere, -cessi, -cessum: I go along, I appear
incendium, -i, n.: fire
incendo, -ere, -cendi, -cēnsum: I set alight, I fire
incido, -ere, -cidi: I fall into, fall onto, I drop into
inclīnātio, ionis, f.: an incline, a swell (of the sea)
inclūdo, -ere, -clūsi, -clūsum: I shut in
incorruptus -a -um: incorrupt
incrēmentum, -i, n.: increase

incurvus, -a -um: curved
inde: thence, then
indico (1): I point out, reveal, inform
indūco, -ere, -dūxi, -ductum: I lead into, I induce
induo, -ere, indui, indūtum: I put on
industria, -ae, f.: energy, industry
inerro (1): I wander among
infēlix, infēlicis: unlucky, unhappy
inferior, inferius: lower, inferior
inferus -a -um: below; di inferi: the gods of the underworld
infirmus -a -um: weak, infirm
inflo (1): I breathe into, blow
ingenium, -i, n.: talents, ability, genius
ingēns, ingentis: huge
ingredior, ingredi, ingressus: I go into, enter
inicio, inicere, -iēci, -iectum: I throw into
initium, -i, n.: a beginning
iniūria, -ae, f.: injury, wrong
innocēns, innocentis: innocent, harmless
inopia, -ae, f.: shortage, lack, want
inquam, inquit: I, he say(s)
īnsapiēns, īnsapientis: foolish
īnsidiae, -ārum, f.: ambush, attack
īnsignis, -e: outstanding, brilliant
īnsisto, -sistere, stiti: I stand on, I urge on
īnstituo, -ere, -stitui, -stitūtum: I set up, I institute, I educate
īnstrūmentum, -i, n.: a tool, an instrument
īnsula, -ae, f.: island
īnsum, inesse, infui: I am in
intellego, -ere, intellēxi, intellēctum: I understand
intereā: meanwhile
interest: it is of importance, it matters
interficio, -ficere, -fēci, -fectum: I kill
interim: meanwhile
interior, interius: inner
intermitto, -ere, -mīsi, -missum: I leave off
interrogo (1): I ask, I question
intervenio, -īre, -vēni, -ventum: I come between, I intervene
interventus, -ūs, m.: intervention
intrā (prep. with acc.): within
intro (1): I enter
introeo, introīre, introii: I enter
inultus -a -um: unavenged
invādo, -ere, -vāsi, -vāsum: I attack
invenio, -īre, -vēni, -ventum: I come upon, find
invictus -a -um: unconquered, unconquerable
invīso, -ere, invīsi: I visit, I go to see

137

invīsus -a -um: hated
invīto (1): I invite
invītus -a -um: unwilling
invius -a -um: trackless
iocor (1): I joke
iocus, -i, m.: a joke
īra, -ae, f.: anger
īrācundus -a -um: prone to anger, irritable
īrrito (1): I rouse to anger, irritate
iste, ista, istud: that
item: likewise
iter, itineris, n.: a journey, a march
iubeo, -ēre, iussi, iussum: I order
iūcundus -a -um: pleasing, delightful
iūdicium, -i, n.: judgement
iūdico (1): I judge
iungo, -ere, iūnxi, iūnctum: I join
iūstus -a -um: just
iūro (1): I swear
iuventus, -tūtis, f.: youth
iuvo, -āre, iūvi, iūtum: I help, I please; iuvat: it please

labor, labōris, m.: work
lābor, lābi, lāpsus: I glide, fall
lacrima, -ae, f.: a tear
lacrimo (1): I cry
lacteus -a -um: milky, full of milk
laetitia, -ae, f.: joy
laetus -a -um: joyful, fruitful
languidus -a -um: sluggish
lapideus -a -um: made of stone
lapis, lapidis, m.: a stone
lar, laris, m.: a spirit of the home; home
largus -a -um: bountiful, generous
lateo (2): I am hidden
latrōcinium, -i, n.: robbery
lātus -a -um: broad, wide
laudo (1): I praise
laus, laudis, f.: praise
lavo, -āre, lāvi, lautum/lōtum: I wash
lectico (1): I read again and again
lectio, lectiōnis, f.: reading
lectus, -i, m.: a bed, a couch
lego, -ere, lēgi, lēctum: I read
lēnis -e: gentle
leo, leōnis, m.: a lion
lētum, -i, n.: death

levis -e: light, slight, trifling
lēx, lēgis, f.: law
libellus, -i, m.: a little book, a note-book
libēns, libentis: glad; libenter: gladly
līber, lībera, līberum: free; līberi, līberōrum: children
līberālis -e: liberal, generous
lībero (1): I free
lībertas, -ātis, f.: freedom
lībertus, -i, m.: a freedman
licet, licēre, licuit: it is allowed, it is lawful (with dative of person);
   tibi licet: you may . . .
lingua, -ae, f.: tongue, language
linquo, -ere, līqui, lictum: I leave
liquēns, liquentis: liquid
litterae, -ārum, f.: a letter, literature
lītus, lītoris, n.: shore
loco (1): I place
locus, -i, m.: a place
longē (adv.): far
loquor, loqui, locūtus: I speak
lōrum, -i, n.: a thong; lōra (pl.): reins
lūceo (2): I give light, shine
luctor (1): I struggle, wrestle
lūctus, -ūs, m.: grief, mourning
lūdo, -ere, lūsi, lūsum: I play
lūdus, -i, m.: a game, a school
lūna, -ae, f.: the moon
lupus, -i, m.: a wolf
lustrum, -i, n.: a den, a lair
lūsus, -ūs, m.: play, amusement
lūx, lūcis, f.: light
luxuria, -ae, f.: excess, luxury

magis: more
magister, magistri, m.: a master
magnitūdo, -tūdinis, f.: size, magnitude
magnus -a -um: great; magna pars: the majority
māiōres, māiōrum: ancestors
maledictum, -i, n.: a curse, abuse
mālo, mālle, mālui: I prefer
mando, -ere: I chew
māne: in the morning
maneo, -ere, mānsi, mānsum: I remain
mānes, mānium: the spirits of the dead
manus, -ūs, f.: hand, a band (of people)
maritīmus -a -um: of the sea, maritime

marītus, -i, m.: a married man, a husband
mātrōna, -ae, f.: a married woman
mātūrus -a -um: early; mature: in good time
medicus, -i, m.: a doctor
mediocris -e: moderate
meditor (1): think over, meditate, compose
medius -a -um: middle
memini, meminisse: I remember
memor, memoris: mindful of, remembering
memoria, -ae, f.: memory
mēns, mentis, f.: mind
mēnsis, mēnsis, m.: a month
mereo (2): I deserve; bene merēns: well deserving
meridiēs, -ēi, f.: midday
meritum, -i, n.: a good deed
merus -a -um: unmixed, pure, mere
mēta, -ae, f.: turning post (on a race track)
metuo, -ere, metui: I fear
metus, -ūs, m.: fear
mīlia, mīlium, n.: thousands, miles
mina, -ae, f.: a threat
ministrātor, -ōris, m.: steward
minitor (1): I threaten
minus: less
minūtus -a -um: tiny, minute
mīror (1): I wonder at, am surprised at
mīrus -a -um: wonderful, surprising
misericordia, -ae, f.: mercy
modestus -a -um: modest
modŏ (adv.): only; lately; modŏ . . . modŏ . . . : now . . . now . . .
modus, -i, m.: way, limit, sort
moenia, moenium, n.: town walls
molestia, -ae, f.: annoyance, vexation, worry
molestus -a -um: annoying; moleste fero: I am annoyed at, vexed by
mollis -e: soft, tender
moneo (2): I warn, advise
morior, mori, mortuus: I die
moror (1): I delay
mors, mortis, f.: death
mōs, mōris, m.: custom
moveo, -ēre, mōvi, mōtum: I move, I start
mulier, mulieris, f.: a woman
multitūdo, -ūdinis, f.: a large number, a multitude
municeps, municipis, c.: a citizen of a municipium
municipium, -i, n.: a municipality, a self-governing town of Roman
    citizens in Italy or the provinces
mūnus, mūneris, n.: a gift, duty, show

murmur, murmuris, n.: a murmur
mūto (1): I change

nactus -a -um: having obtained (past participle of nancīscor)
namque = nam: for
narro (1): I tell a story, relate, say
nāscor, nāsci, nātus: I am born
nātio, nātiōnis, f.: tribe
nato (1): I swim
nātūra, -ae, f.: nature
nātus, -i, m.: a son
nausea, -ae, f.: sickness, nausea
nāvigo (1): I sail
nāvis, nāvis, f.: a ship
nē . . . quidem: not even
necessārius -a -um: necessary
necesse est: it is necessary
neco (1): I kill
nefārius -a -um: wicked
neglegentia, -ae, f.: carelessness, negligence
nego (1): I deny
negōtior (1): I conduct business
negōtium, -i, n.: business
nēmo, nēminem: no one
nemus, nemoris, n.: a wood
nepos, nepōtis, m.: a grandchild
nēscio, -īre, nēscii, nēscīvi: I do not know
nimius -a -um: too much, excessive
nimis (adv.): too much, too
nitidus -a -um: shining
nōbilis -e: well-born, well-known
noctū: by night
nōlo, nōlle, nōlui: I am unwilling, I refuse
nōmen, nōminis, n.: a name
nōndum: not yet
nōnnumquam: sometimes
nōsco, nōscere, nōvi, nōtum: I get to know; nōvi: I know
nōtus -a -um: well-known
novus -a -um: new
nox, noctis, f.: night
nūbes, nūbis, f.: cloud
nūbo, -ere, nūpsi, nūptum: I marry
nūdo (1): I bare, strip
numero (1): I count
numerus, -i, m.: number
nūntio (1): I announce
nūper: lately

11

obeo, obīre, obii, obitum: I go to meet, I meet, I fulfil
oblecto (1): I delight
obligo (1): I bind, I oblige
obscēnus -a -um: obscene
obsecro (1): I beseech
obsto, obstāre, obstiti: I stand in the way of, block, hold up
obscūrus -a -um: dark, obscure
obtineo, -ēre, -tinui, -tentum: I hold, obtain
occāsio, -iōnis, f.: opportunity
occīdo, -ere, -cīdi, -cīsum: I kill
occupātio, -iōnis, f.: occupation
occupo (1): I seize, I occupy
occurro, -ere, occurri, occursum: I run to meet, occur (to mind)
Ōceanus, -i, m.: the Ocean
ocellus, -i, m.: little eye, eye
oculārius, -i, m.: an oculist
oculus, -i, m.: an eye
odium, -i, n.: hatred
offero, offerre, obtuli, oblātum: I offer
officium, -i, n.: duty
ōlim: once upon a time, at some time
omnīno: altogether
omnis -e: all
onero (1): I burden, load
onus, oneris, n.: burden, load
operio, -īre, operui, opertum: I close
oportet, oportēre, oportuit: it behoves; mē oportet: I should
oppidum, i, n.: a town
opportūnus -a -um: convenient, opportune
opprimo, -ere, oppressi, oppressum: I oppress, weigh down
(ops) opis, f.: help; opēs, opum: wealth, resources
opus, operis, n.: work; opus est (with abl.): there is need of
orātio, -iōnis, f.: a speech
orbis, orbis, m.: circle
ōrdo, ōrdinis, m.: order, rank
orior, orīri, ortus: I arise
ōro (1): I pray
ōs, ōris, n.: mouth, face
osculum, -i, n.: a kiss
ostendo, -ere, ostendi, ostentum: I show, point out
ōtiōsus -a -um: leisurely, at leisure, idle
ōtium, -i, n.: leisure, idleness
ōvum, -i, n.: an egg

paene: almost
pāgus, -i, m.: village

pallidus -a -um: pale
palma, -ae, f.: palm, prize
pānis, pānis, m.: bread
parco, -ere, peperci, parsum: I spare (with dative)
pāreo (2): I obey (with dative)
pariter: equally
paro (1): I prepare
pars, partis, f.: part
parum: too little
parvulus -a -um: small, little
passus, ūs, m.: a pace, step
patefacio, -facere, -fēci, -factum: I open, I reveal
pateo (2): I am open; patēns, patentis: open
patior, pati, passus: I suffer, I allow; patiēns, patientis: enduring,
    patient
patrius -a -um: of one's father, of one's fatherland
pauci, -ae, -a: few
paulum: a little
pauper, pauperis: poor
pavidus -a -um: trembling
pavīmentum, -i, n.: pavement, floor
pāx, pācis, f.: peace
pectus, pectoris, n.: breast, heart
pecūnia, -ae, f.: money
pecus, pecoris, n.: flock, herd
pedes, peditis, c.: on foot, a foot soldier
pello, -ere, pepuli, pulsum: I drive
penātes, penātium, m.: the gods of the household
pendeo, -ēre, pependi, pēnsum: I hang, I depend on
pepuli: past tense of pello
perago, -ere, perēgi, perāctum: I complete
percontor (1): I question
percutio, -cutere, -cussi, -cussum: I strike
perdo, -ere, perdidi, perditum: I lose, waste, destroy
pereo, perīre, perii, peritum: I perish
perficio, -ficere, -fēci, -fectum: I achieve, complete; perfice ut: see
    that . . .
perīculum, -i, n.: danger
permitto, -ere, -mīsi, -missum: I permit, leave
perquīro, -ere: I search for
persono, -āre, -sonui: I resound
persuādeo, -ēre, -suāsi, -suāsum: I persuade (with dative)
pertimeo (2): I am very frightened
pervenio, -īre, -vēni, -ventum: I arrive at, reach
pervinco, -ere, -vīci, -victum: I conquer, I prevail
pes, pedis, m.: foot
peto, -ere, petīvi/petii, petītum: I seek, I ask, I make for

143

pinguis -e: rich, fat
piscis, piscis, m.: a fish
piscor (1): I fish
pius -a -um: loyal, loving, pious
placeo (2): I please (with dative): mihi placet: it pleases me, I am resolved
plāco (1): I placate
plānē: clearly
plēbs, plēbis, f.: the people
plēnus -a -um: full, full of
plērīque, plēraeque, plēraque: most, a good many, several
plūs: more; plus minus: more or less
poena, -ae, f.: punishment, penalty
pōmum, -i, n.: fruit
pondus, ponderis, n.: weight
pōno, -ere, posui, positum: I place, set up
porta, -ae, f.: a gate
posco, -ere, poposci: I demand
possum, posse, potui: I am able, I can
posterus -a -um: next
posteā: afterwards
posthac: hereafter
postis, postis, m.: a gate post, a gate
postrēmo: lastly
postridiē: on the next day
postulātio, -iōnis, f.: a demand
potestās, -ātis, f.: power
potius: rather (comparative adv.)
potissimum: best of all (superlative adv.)
prae (prep. with abl.): because of
praebeo (2): I offer, I show, I provide
praeceps, praecipitis: headlong
praecipuē: especially
praeceptor, -ōris, m.: teacher
praeda, -ae, f.: booty, plunder
praedūrus -a -um: hard
praemium, -i, n.: reward, prize
praesertim: especially
praesidium, -i, n.: protection
praesto, -stāre, -stiti: I excel; me praesto: I show myself
praeter (prep. with acc.): besides, except
praetereā: moreover
praetereo, -īre, -ii, -itum: I pass by, overtake
prātum, -i, n.: a meadow
precēs, precum, f.: prayers
precor (1): I pray
premo, -ere, pressi, pressum: I press

144

pridiē: the day before
prīmus -a -um: first; prīmo, prīmum (adv.): at first, firstly
princeps, principis, m.: leader, chief; the emperor
priusquam: before (conjunction)
privātim: privately
prō (prep. with abl.): in front of; on behalf of; instead of
probitas, -atis, f.: goodness, uprightness
probus -a -um: good, upright
prōcēdo, -ere, -cessi, -cessum: I advance, go forward, proceed
prōcumbo, -ere, -cubui, -cubitum: I lie down
prōdo, -ere, -didi, -ditum: I betray
proelior (1): I battle, fight
proficīscor, -ficīsci, -fectus: I set out
profundus -a -um: deep, high
prōgredior, - gredi, -gressus: I advance
prohibeo (2): I prevent
promitto, -ere, -mīsi, -missum: I promise
prope (prep. with acc. and adv.): near
propero (1): I hasten
propinquitās, -ātis, f.: nearness (of place or blood)
prōpositus -a -um: intended, proposed
propter (prep. with acc.): on account of
prosperus -a -um: successful, prosperous
proximus -a -um: nearest, next
prūdentia, -ae, f.: good sense, wisdom, prudence
pūblicus -a -um: public; pūblicē: publicly, at public expense
pudīcitia, -ae, f.: chastity, purity
pudor, pudōris, m.: modesty
puer, pueri, m.: a boy, a slave
puerīlis -e: boyish, childish
pugillāris, pugillāris, m.: a writing tablet
pulcher, pulchra, pulchrum: beautiful
pūrus -a -um: pure
puto (1): I think

quā: where
quadriiugus -a -um: yoked in fours
quadrirēmus, -i, m.: a quadrireme (a ship with four banks of oars)
quaero, -ere, quaesīvi/quaesii, quaesītum: I ask, I look for, I gain
quaeso, -ere: I ask
quālis -e: of what kind, such as
quam: than; how
quamvīs: although
quārē: therefore
quasī: as if, like
quemadmodum: how; as
querēla, -ae, f.: complaint

queror, queri, questus: I complain
quia: because
quīcumque, quaecumque, quodcumque: whoever, whatever
quīdam, quaedam, quoddam: a certain
quidem: indeed; nē . . . quidem: not even
quies, quiētis, f.: rest, quiet
quiēsco, -ere, quiēvi, quiētum: I rest
quīnam? quaenam? quodnam? who? what?
Quirītes, Quirītium, m.: the Roman citizens
quis? quid? who? what?
quis, quid: anyone, anything
quisquam, quicquam: anyone, anything (after a negative)
quisque, quicque: each
quisquis, quidquid: whoever, whatever
quo: whither
quocircā: and so; for this reason
quoniam: since
quoque: also
quot (indecl. adj.): how many
quotiēns/quoties: how often; toties . . . quoties . . .: as often as
quotiēnscumque: however often, whenever

rapidus -a -um: rushing, tearing
rāro: rarely
ratio, ratiōnis, f.: reason, idea, account, way, accounts, sums
recipio, -cipere, -cēpi, -ceptum: I take back, receive, accept
recordātio, -iōnis, f.: memory, remembrance
recordor (1): I remember
recreātus -a -um: recovered, revived
rēctus -a -um: straight, right; recte: rightly
recubo, -āre, -cubui, -cubitum: I lie down again, go back to bed
recurro, -ere, -curri, -cursum: I run back
recūso (1): I refuse
reddo, -ere, -reddidi, redditum: I give back, return, give what is
    due, pay
redeo, redīre, redii, reditum: I go back
redigo, -ere, redēgi, redāctum: I reduce, bring under
redimo, -ere, redēmi, redēmptum: I buy back, buy off
refero, -ferre, -ttuli, -lātum: I carry back; I report; I refer back
reficio, -ficere, -fēci, -fectum: I remake, repair, recover
rēgīna, -ae, f.: queen
regio, regiōnis, f.: district, region
rēgius -a -um: royal
rēgnum, -i, n.: kingdom, rule
rego, -ere, rēxi, rēctum: I rule, command
regredior, -gredi, -gressus: I return
religio, -iōnis, f.: religion, superstition

146

relinquo, -ere, -līqui, -lictum: I leave behind
relīquus -a -um: remaining
remitto, -ere, -mīsi, -missum: I send back; I remit
removeo, -ere, -mōvi, -mōtum: I remove
rēmus, -i, m.: oar
repente: suddenly
reperio, -īre, repperi, repertum: I find
repleo, -ēre, replēvi, replētum: I fill, satisfy
repōno, -ere, -posui, -positum: I lay down
reporto (1): I bring back
reprehendo, -ere, -prehendi, -prehēnsum: I blame
repudio (1): I reject
reputo (1): I think over, reflect
requies, requiētis, f.: rest
requīro, -ere, -quisīvi/quisii, -quisītum: I ask, I look for, I miss
resolvo, -ere, -solvi, -solūtum: I unfasten, I release
respicio, -spicere, -spexi, -spectum: I look back at
respondeo, -ēre, -spondi, -spōnsum: I reply
restituo, -ere, -stitui, -stitūtum: I restore
resto (1): I remain, I am left
retraho, -ere, -trāxi, -tractum: I drag back
retro: backwards
revoco (1): I recall, call back
renovo (1): I renew
rīdeo, -ēre, rīdi, rīsum: I laugh, I smile
rigidus -a -um: hard
rōbur, rōboris, n.: oak; strength
rogo (1): I ask, I ask for
rota, -ae, f.: a wheel
ruīna, -ae, f.: collapse, ruin
rumpo, -ere, rūpi, ruptum: I break
ruo, -ere, rui: I rush
rūrsus: again
rūs, rūris, n.: country; rura: farm, estate
rūsticus -a -um: of the country, rustic

sacer, sacra, sacrum: sacred
saepe: often
saltem: at least
salūs, salūtis, f.: safety; health; greeting
salūto (1): I greet, I pay respects to
salvē, salvēte, greetings! (imperatives of salveo)
salvus -a -um: safe
sānctus -a -um: holy; righteous
sanguis, sanguinis, m.: blood
sānus -a -um: sane

satis: enough
saxum, -i, n.: a rock
scelerātus -a -um: wicked, criminal
scelus, sceleris, n.: a crime
scio, scīre, scii/scīvi, scītum: I know
scrībo, -ere, scrīpsi, scrīptum: I write
scūtum, -i, n.: a shield
seco, -āre, secui, sectum: I cut
sēcūrus -a -um: free from care, not caring
sedeo, -ēre, sēdi, sessum: I sit
sēdēs, sēdis, f.: a seat, a home
segnis -e: slack, lingering
semel: once
semper: always
sempiternus -a -um: everlasting
senecta, -ae, f.: old age
senex, senis, m.: an old man
sēnsus, -ūs, m.: feeling
sententia, -ae, f.: opinion, vote
sentio, -īre, sēnsi, sēnsum: I feel, preceive
sequor, sequi, secūtus: I follow
serēnus -a -um: fine, serene
sermo, sermōnis, m.: conversation, talk, language
sēro: late
servio (4): I am a slave, I serve (with dative)
servitūs, -ūtis, f.: slavery
servo (1): I save, I guard, I watch
siccus -a -um: dry; siccum, -i, n.: dry land
sīcut/sīcuti: just as
sīdus, sīderis, n.: a star, constellation
signum, -i, n.: a sign, signal
silentium, -i, n.: silence
silva, -ae, f.: a wood
similis -e: like to, similar
simplex, simplicis: simple, straightforward
simul: at the same time; simul ac: as soon as
simulo (1): I pretend
sīn: but if
sine (prep. with abl.) without
singulus -a -um: single, separate
sinister, sinistra, sinistrum: left
situs -a -um: buried, laid
sīve . . . sīve . . .: whether . . . or . . .
socius -a -um: ally, friend, companion
sōl, sōlis, m.: the sun
solācium, -i, n.: comfort
soleo, -ēre, solitus: I am accustomed to

148

solitūdo, solitūdinis, f.: loneliness, solitude
sollicito (1): I worry
sollicitus -a -um: worried
sōlor (1): I comfort, console
sŏlum, -i, n.: the ground, soil
sōlum (adv.): only
sōlus -a -um: only, sole
solvo, -ere, solvi, solūtum: I loose, I free, I pay: navem solvo: I set sail
somnus, -i, m.: sleep
sonipēs, sonipedis, m.: a horse
sonus, -i, m.: a sound
sordidus -a -um: dirty, mean
sors, sortis, f.: lot, chance
spatiōsus -a -um: spatious, broad
spatium, -i, n.: space
spargo, -ere, sparsi, sparsum: I scatter
spectāculum, -i, n.: a show
specto (1): I look at, watch
sperno, -ere, sprēvi, sprētum: I despise
spēs, spēi, f.: hope
spōnsātus -a -um: betrothed
statim: at once
statua, -ae, f.: a statue
sto, stāre, steti, statum: I stand, I stand still
stringo, -ere, strinxi, strictum: I graze; I draw (a sword)
studeo (2): I am keen on, I support, I study
studiōsus -a -um: keen, studious, curious
studium, -i, n.: keenness; study
suādeo, -ēre, suāsi, suāsum: I persuade (with dative)
subeo, subīre, subii, subitum: I go under; I undergo; I go up to
subiaceo, -ēre, -iacui: I lie beneath
subicio, -icere, -iēci, -iectum: I throw under, throw beneath
subito: suddenly
subitus -a -um: sudden
sublātus -a -um: see tollo
subvenio, -īre, -vēni, -ventum: I come to help (with dative)
succēdo, -ere, -cessi, -cessum: I enter into
sufficio, -ficere, -fēci, -fectum: I suffice; sufficit: it is enough
sūmo, -ere, sūmpsi, sūmptum: I take, I adopt
sūmptus, -ūs, m.: expense
superbus -a -um: proud
superior, superius: superior, higher
supersum, superesse, superfui: I survive, I am left
superus -a -um: above; superi (di): the gods above
supprimo, -ere, -pressi, -pressum: I suppress
suprā (adv.): above, on top
suprēmus -a -um: last

surgo, -ere, surrēxi, surrectum: I arise
sus, suis, c.: a pig
suspicio, suspicere, suspexi, suspectum: I suspect
suspicio, -ionis, f.: suspicion
sustuli: see tollo
taceo (2): I am silent
tacitus -a -um: silent, quiet
tam: so
tamquam: as if
tandem: at length
tango, -ere, tetigi, tāctum: I touch
tantum: only
tantus -a -um: so great
tardus -a -um: slow, late
tego, -ere, tēxi, tēctum: I cover, I protect
tellūs tellūris, f.: earth
tēlum, -i, n.: a (thrown) weapon
temperantia, -ae, f.: restraint, temperance
tempestās, -ātis, f.: storm, tempest
tempus, temporis, n.: time; tempore: in good time
tendo, -ere, tetendi, tentum: I stretch, pull
tenebrae, arum, f.: darkness
teneo, -ēre, tenui, tentum: I hold
tener, tenera, tenerum: tender
tenuis -e: small, fine
ter: three times
tergum, -i, n.: back
tero, -ere, trīvi, trītum: I rub, I grind
terra, -ae, f.: a land; earth
terreo (2): I terrify
thēsaurus, -i, m.: treasure
timeo (2): I fear
timidus -a -um: fearful, timid
tolero (1): I endure
tollo, -ere, sustuli, sublātum: I raise, remove, destroy
tono (1): I thunder
torqueo, -ēre, torsi, tortum: I twist, I torture
tot (indecl. adj.): so many
toties: so often; toties . . . quoties: as often as
tōtus -a -um: whole
trādo, -ere, tradidi, traditum: I hand over
traho, -ere, trāxi, tractum: I draw, I drag
traicio, traicere, traieci, traiectum: I pierce
trānseo, -īre, -ii, -itum: I cross, I pass
trānsfero, -ferre, -tuli, -lātum: I carry across, I transfer, I move
trānsmitto, -ere, -mīsi, -missum: I pass, overtake
tremo, -ere, tremui: I tremble

trepido (1): I panic
trepidus -a -um: panic stricken
tribūnal, tribunālis, n.: a platform, tribunal
tribuo, -ere, tribui, tribūtum: I give, grant
tribūtum, -i, n.: tribute
trīclinium, -i, n.: dining room
trīstis -e: sad, severe
tueor, tuēri, tuitus: I gaze at, I guard
tumultuōsus -a -um: riotous
tumultus -ūs, m.: uproar, riot, turmoil
turba, -ae, f.: a crowd
turbo (1): I disturb, upset
turpis -e: base, disgraceful
tūtus -a -um: safe

ulmus, -i, f.: an elm tree
ultimus -a -um: last
ultio, ultiōnis, f.: vengeance
umbra, -ae, f.: a shadow
umerus, -i, m.: shoulder
unā: together with
unda, -ae, f.: a wave
unde: whence, from where
undique: from all sides
unicē: uniquely
ūniversus -a -um: altogether, all
unquam: ever
urbānus -a -um: of the city; urbane, witty
uro, -ere, ussi, ustum: I burn
usquam: anywhere
usque; continually; usque ad: right up to, all the way to
uter, utra, utrum: which (of two)? utrum . . . an? whether . . . or?
uti = ut
ūtilis -e: useful
utinam: oh that . . . ! (introduces a wish)
ūtor, ūti, ūsus: I use (with ablative)
uxor, uxōris, f.: a wife

vacuus -a -um: empty, free from
vādo, -ere: I go
vadum, -i, n.: a strait; vada, vadorum: shallows
valdē: extremely
valē, valētē: goodbye (imperatives of valeo)
valēns, valentis: strong, healthy
valeo, (2): I am strong, I am healthy
valētūdo, -ūdinis, f.: health; bad health

validus -a -um: strong
vallis, vallis, f.: a valley
vānus -a -um: empty, vain
varius -a -um: varied, different
vastus -a -um: vast, endless
velōcitās, -ātis, f.: speed
velōx, velōcis: fast
venātio, -iōnis, f.: hunting
vēndo, -ere, vēndidi, vēnditum: I sell
vēnor (1): I hunt
ventus, -i, m.: wind
venustus -a -um: lovely, charming
verbero (1): I lash, beat
verbum, -i, n.: a word
verbus, verberis, n.: a lash; verbera, verberum: blows
vereor (2): I fear, I respect
vēro: indeed
vērum: but
vērus -a -um: true
versus, -ūs, m.: verse
verto, -ere, verti, versum: I turn, I change
vespera, -ae, f.: evening
vestīgium, -i, n.: trace, track, foot-print
vestīmentum, -i, n.: clothing
vestis, vestis, m.: clothing
veto, -āre, vetui, vetitum: I forbid
vetus, veteris: old
vexo (1): I harass
via, -ae, f.: a road, way
viātor, viatōris, m.: a traveller, passer by
vīcīnus -a -um: neighbouring
victor, victōris, m.: conqueror, victor
video, -ēre, vīdi, vīsum: I see; videor: I seem
villa, -ae, f.: a country house; a farm
vincio, -īre, vinxi, vinctum: I bind
vinco, -ere, vīci, victum: I conquer, I win
vinculum, -i, n.: chain, bonds
vīnum, -i, n.: wine
violēns, violentis: violent
vir, viri, m.: a man, a husband
virgo, virginis, f.: a girl, a maiden
virīlis -e: manly
virtus, virtūtis, f.: courage, virtue
vīs, (vim): force, vīres, vīrium: strength
vīso, vīsere, vīsi: I visit, I come to see
vīta, -ae, f.: life
vitium, -i, n.: a fault

152

vīvidus -a -um: lively
vīvo, -ere, vīxi, vīctum: I live
vīvus -a -um: living, alive
vix: scarcely
vocātus, -ūs, m.: a summons
voco (1): I call
volo, velle, volui: I wish, I am willing
volo (1): I fly
voluptas, -ātis, f.: pleasure
volvo, -ere, volvi, volūtum: I roll
vōtum, -i, n.: a vow, a prayer, a wish
vulgus, -i, n: crowd
vulnus, vulneris, n.: a wound
vultus, -ūs, m.: face, expression